SMALL SOLAR BUILDINGS
in cool northern climates

SMALL SOLAR BUILDINGS
in cool northern climates

David Oppenheim

THE ARCHITECTURAL PRESS LTD

Contents

First published in 1981 by
The Architectural Press Ltd: London

© David Oppenheim 1981

ISBN 0 85139 596 1

**Filmset in Univers and Printed in
Great Britain by Mackays of Chatham Ltd.**

1 The Palm House at Kew, London. The architect was Decimus Burton and the engineer Richard Turner. 1845—48.

This book was written to fill a communication gap. A wealth of information is available on solar energy technology and its applications; such information can range from the most earthy alternative approaches to the most detailed and intricate scientific researches. Yet for members of the building design team and interested non-technical members of the public there is a lack of material that simply presents an overview of what approaches are available, and what has already been *built* in Britain. Even if the possibilities afforded by solar technology intrigue him, the building designer cannot generally afford the time nor mental energy to become involved in it. He feels excluded by a theoretical lack of knowledge and the practical problem of how to implement his interest.

This exclusion is strongly felt in the cool northern climates of Europe. With a cloud cover that seems to preclude solar feasibility, scepticism is rife.

This book therefore was written with five distinct and discrete aims in mind:

- to communicate to non-technical people interested in solar energy.

- to provide concise information that is amply illustrated.

- to highlight the emergence of a new professional, the solar engineer.

- to explain how the building designer works with the solar engineer, and to illustrate the basic solar design principles, sufficient for the building designer to interact successfully with the solar engineer.

- to catalogue all the occupied buildings in Britain that have solar assisted space heating.

In the interests of clarity many ideas and concepts have been reduced to basics. It is hoped that once these have been grasped, the wealth of variety and refinement that exists will be enjoyed by curious and interested building designers and non-technical people.

My acknowledgements are many. Firstly to my friends and colleagues at Solar Energy Developments, London, for providing not only a positive and enthusiastic atmosphere in which to work and learn, but also a pooled body of knowledge and experience that has been invaluable. Secondly to all the people involved in Chapter 10 for their much valued time and patience. And lastly to all the people in the solar fraternity whose open mindedness, basic goodness and enthusiasm make this such a delightful field to work in.

Introduction

Most building designers, as well as the public in general, are sceptical of solar energy technology.

While few know what it means or how it works, most would concede that at the time of the Arab oil embargo of 1973 it promised to be one of the Messiahs leading us to energy salvation. Over the past six years, however, the hopes of the European population in general have evaporated and been replaced by sceptical indifference. Even though solar energy was being harnessed in America, the cloudy intermittent climate of northern Europe **(2)** seemed to preclude any such economic development and this attitude was borne out by the apparently small number of examples being built.

Over those six years however much has changed. In England, there has been the formation of the UK International Solar Energy Society (1973), the creation of the Solar Trade Association (1974), and the emergence of professional architects and engineers who now have repeated experience in both the theory and the actual practice of integrating solar energy technology into buildings. In Britain alone there are between 5—15,000 solar domestic hot water installations (estimates vary), 2—4,000 solar swimming pool installations (estimates vary again), as well as nearly thirty buildings that utilise solar energy to assist in heating their living spaces.

Much of the technology involved initially was developed in Europe, but recently American technology has come to the fore. However, the application of this American solar technology is not always appropriate to northern European climates. Firstly, most of Europe lies to the north of America, and therefore it generally receives less solar radiation; (London only receives 54 per cent of the solar radiation over the winter period compared to New York, and only 36 per cent compared to Los Angeles); secondly, even though it lies well north, many parts of Europe have a temperate climate instead of a cold one because of the presence of the Gulf Stream **(3)**; and thirdly in Britain it is common practice to shut down the heating system overnight, a rare event in the U.S., and such a heating policy is not conducive to favourable solar economics.

In order to assist the building designer in the implementation of solar energy technology, a new professional has emerged; the solar engineer **(4)**. The consultancy is the same as that of a heating and ventilating engineer, except that the solar engineer provides a heating and ventilating service that includes the integration of solar energy technology. He can advise on the most appropriate system, size it, put it out to tender and supervise its construction. What is required of the building designer is that he is aware of all the solar design tools available to him, and be able to decide (with the assistance of the solar engineer) the most appropriate system for a particular project.

2 The Wallasey School beneath a cloudy British sky that seems to preclude solar feasibility.

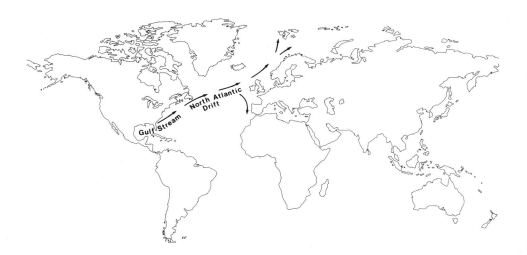

3 The Gulf Stream warms the western seaboard of Europe.

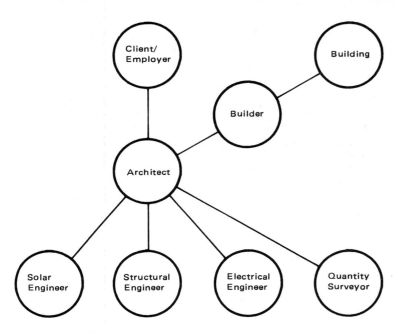

4 The solar engineer is the new professional consultant who provides solar expertise in the traditional consultant framework.

There are many misconceptions regarding solar technology

- *solar does not work because it always needs auxiliary heating:* solar systems rarely attempt to satisfy all of the heating load, and the auxiliary heating system is an integral part of the overall concept. What solar systems do achieve is a reduction in the amount of back up fuel used.

- *solar is not economic:* solar economics are marginal and essentially swap future payments of fuel bills for a once-off capital investment for a solar system. Solar heaters for swimming pools have payback periods in the region of five years. Solar heaters for domestic hot water systems have payback periods in the region of five to fifteen years. Solar assisted space heating systems have no established payback periods because of the lack of extensive documentation, but individual cases have payback periods between seven and twenty years. Natural gas, solar's most common competitor, is not available to every building (the Gas Board estimated they will peak at about sixteen million dwellings supplied, out of the total twenty million existing) and solar economics are far more favourable when compared to oil or electricity rather than to gas.

- *solar in England?* Built and documented examples prove that solar energy is feasible and economic in England.

- *solar energy; "that's the panels on the roof":* Solar panels on the roof are only one way to collect solar energy. Greenhouses collect solar energy. Houses with large south facing windows collect solar energy. Heat pumps (air-conditioners in reverse) take solar energy stored outside (in air, the ground or water) and transfer it to inside.

- *solar panels are for domestic hot water systems:* Solar systems can be used to heat both air and water for space heating. Such solar systems have been used in British homes, schools, exhibition halls, old peoples homes, swimming pools, offices and some industrial applications. There are very few building types or system applications where solar energy cannot make a contribution.

Despite the range of applications already achieved, solar technology has not gained public credibility. The discussion and catalogue that follow in the next nine chapters attempt to dispel the doubts and queries of the sceptical public, in an effort to achieve that credibility.

Climate

This chapter concludes with a crude index that can be used to compare roughly different locations for solar viability.

INTRODUCTION

To all appearances, northern Europe does not seem a likely candidate for integration of solar energy technology. It is cloudy, it is well north and has long winters with short days. Is it then possible to quantify such a climate?

SOLAR BELT AREAS

Places where solar energy is highly viable are called solar belt areas. They have the following characteristics:

- clear winter skies (to maximise the input of solar energy)

- long winters (to write off capital costs more quickly)

- moderate winters (since collector losses become intolerable in very cold weather)

- high fuel costs (to make the price of solar energy more competitive).

New Mexico in the US is such a *solar belt area* with its clear winter skies and plentiful sunshine **(5)**.

The map **(6)** shows the amount of average daily solar radiation available in mid-winter (January in the northern hemisphere and July in the southern hemisphere) throughout the world. It is interesting to note that the US (excluding Alaska and Hawaii) roughly receives between 0.8 and 4.1 kWh/m^2 per average mid-winter day, Australia between 1.5 and 5.5 kWh/m^2, France between 0.8 and 2.0 kWh/m^2, while the United Kingdom receives only about 0.3 to 0.7 kWh/m^2 on an average January day.

INDEX

A crude solar viability index can be obtained for any particular location by comparing the *solar radiation available* and the *space heating load* required to be satisfied.

Such a dimensionless index can be calculated as below:

$$\text{Index} = \frac{\text{Solar radiation available}}{\text{Space heating load}}$$

5   Solar belt areas generally have clear winter skies with plentiful sunshine, as in New Mexico, U.S.A. This is architect David Wright's first house built in Santa Fe in 1974.

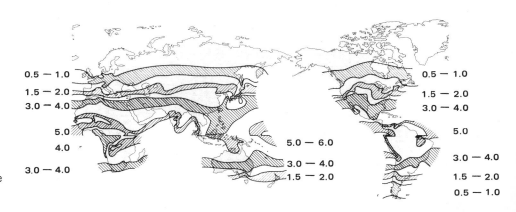

6   Solar radiation map for winter showing January figures for the Northern hemisphere and July figures for the Southern hemisphere. Source: Lof, Duffie and Smith, *World Distribution of Solar Radiation.* Units in kWh/m^2 per day on a horizontal surface.

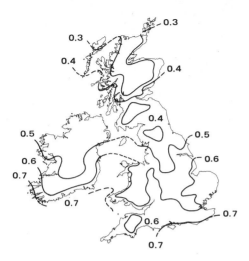

7 Average daily total of solar radiation received on a horizontal surface in January (kWh/m^2).

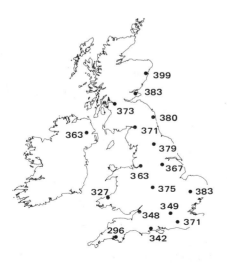

8 Average degree day figures for January.

SOLAR RADIATION AVAILABLE

The sun's radiation is received in three ways:

- *direct radiation* — light that casts a shadow direct from the sun
- *diffuse radiation* — non-shadow-casting light from the whole sky vault
- *reflected radiation* — direct or diffuse radiation that bounces off objects

Cloudless days provide the most solar radiation, but even totally cloudy days can provide useful radiation (up to about one third of that available on a cloudless day at the same time of the year).

In Britain, the Meteorological Office at Bracknell provides maps that show average daily totals of *global radiation* (direct plus diffuse radiation) on a monthly basis.

Illustration **(7)** shows the map for January, indicating that the south of Britain receives about twice the amount of radiation on a horizontal surface when compared to the north of Britain.

SPACE HEATING LOAD

The space heating load of a standard building in different locations is proportional to the *degree days* of that location.

Tables documenting *degree days* for Britain can be obtained from the Department of Energy, such as its publication "Fuel efficiency booklet 7 : Degree Days" which defines and explains the concept of *degree days*, as well as tabulating the 22-year mean figures for the seventeen regions of the United Kingdom.

Illustration **(8)** shows the January *degree days* for the seventeen regions: sadly no "contour" maps exist for each month.

Essentially, the *degree day* is the daily difference in ^{O}C between a base temperature of 15.5^{O}C and the 24-hour mean outside temperature (when it falls below the base temperature). Thus if on one day the 24-hour mean outside temperature was 2.5^{O}C then the number of degree days for that day would be 15.5^{O}C–2.5^{O}C, equalling *13*. By adding the daily totals for one particular month (ie 13 plus 16 plus 12 etc), the *monthly degree day total* is obtained (for example 349 for January in the Thames Valley region). By adding the monthly totals over an entire heating season (say September to May), the *heating season degree day total* can be obtained (for example 2030 for the Thames Valley region).

CRUDE SOLAR VIABILITY INDEX

Table **(9)** lists the *crude solar viability indices* for stations in the seventeen degree day regions, computed by dividing the **solar radiation available** by the **degree days** for each particular month. A heating season total for each location is also given.

It can be seen from map **(10)**, as might well be expected, that the most favourable areas lie to the south of Britain, and the least favourable areas to the north. A more detailed study involving far more parameters (by Professor J.K. Page at Sheffield University) is soon to be published and will provide more accurate results.

		Sept	Oct	Nov	Dec	Jan	Feb	Mar	Apr	May	Total
1	Thames Valley	50.0	12.5	3.1	1.4	1.6	3.6	8.1	16.1	38.1	134.5
2	South Eastern	36.3	11.2	3.6	1.4	1.8	3.9	8.1	15.8	31.5	113.6
3	Southern	41.6	13.2	4.1	1.8	2.0	4.9	8.8	18.1	35.5	130.0
4	South Western	51.7	13.9	3.7	1.8	2.0	4.4	8.9	17.8	35.1	139.3
5	Severn Valley	41.7	11.9	3.3	1.6	1.8	3.8	8.2	16.1	35.4	123.8
6	Midland	28.0	8.7	2.4	1.2	1.5	3.1	6.2	12.8	26.8	90.7
7	West Pennines	33.5	9.9	2.6	1.5	1.4	3.2	7.1	14.2	31.3	104.7
8	North Western	25.6	8.1	2.2	0.8	1.2	3.2	6.2	13.3	23.9	84.9
9	Borders	22.2	7.3	2.3	1.0	1.2	3.1	5.7	12.3	20.2	75.3
10	North Eastern	27.3	8.2	2.4	1.1	1.2	3.0	6.3	12.8	25.8	88.1
11	East Pennines	32.5	9.6	2.8	1.1	1.4	3.1	6.6	13.9	29.5	100.5
12	East Anglia	40.5	11.4	3.5	1.8	1.7	3.8	7.1	13.8	32.2	115.8
13	West Scotland	21.9	7.0	2.0	0.8	1.1	3.1	6.0	13.4	23.5	78.8
14	East Scotland	23.6	7.6	2.1	0.9	1.1	3.1	5.5	12.7	20.2	76.8
15	North East Scotland	18.6	6.3	1.7	0.7	0.9	2.9	5.3	11.9	18.6	66.9
16	Wales	42.5	12.3	3.4	1.6	1.8	4.3	8.8	16.5	31.8	123.0
17	Northern Ireland	27.0	7.8	2.4	1.1	1.2	3.7	6.8	15.0	24.8	89.8

9 Crude solar viability indices

INTERPRETATION

This crude solar viability index should only be interpreted as indicating degrees of difficulty. The higher the index the easier it will be to make the system viable. Since examples exist all over Britain and the Continent, an area with a low index should not discourage a designer, but rather sharpen his wits to the problems ahead.

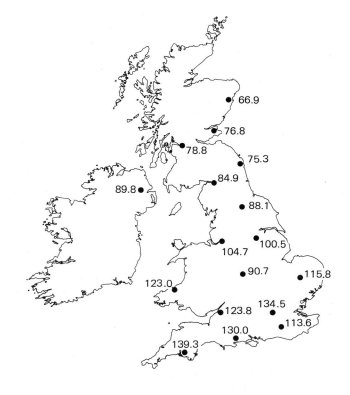

10 Map showing crude solar viability indices for whole heating season

EUROPEAN INDEX

At the time of writing the author is not aware of any published work that indicates a solar viability index for Europe, though work being done both in England and on the Continent should be available in the near future.

Illustration **(11)** is an overlay of two parameters that together give an indication of approximate subdivisions for Europe relating to solar viability.

The first parameter is *global radiation* for January indicated by three isolines; 0.5 kWh/m^2 per day, 1.0 kWh/m^2 per day and 2.0 kWh/m^2 per day.

The second parameter is a division into *mild and cold winters*, based on the maps produced by the late Professor D.L. Linton.

For reference, five cities in the US have been plotted alongside to show their relative latitudes.

From **(11)** it can be seen, as expected, that the climate gets more severe from west to east (except for the pocket of cold winter around the Pyrennes and northern Spain) and sunnier from north to south.

Once again, the interpretation of **(11)** should be seen as indicating degrees of difficulty, rather than showing viable or non-viable areas. With all other considerations equal, however, cold sunny winter climates, such as the Pyrennes or the Northern Appenines should result in *more viable* solar assisted space heating schemes, than could dull winter climes that exist in, say, Latvia.

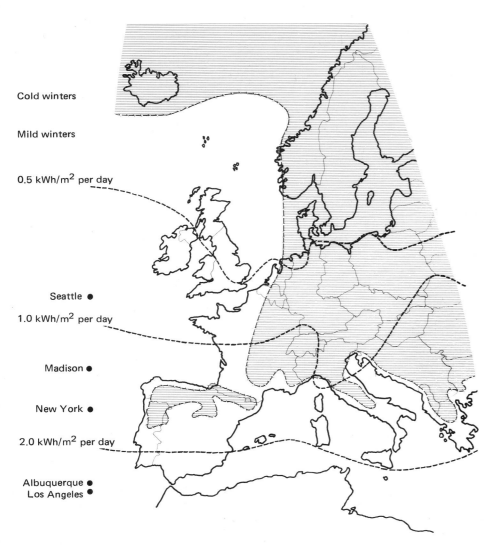

Cold winters

Mild winters

0.5 kWh/m^2 per day

Seattle ●

1.0 kWh/m^2 per day

Madison ●

New York ●

2.0 kWh/m^2 per day

Albuquerque ●
Los Angeles ●

11 Map showing division of mild and cold winters for Europe, superimposed on global radiation isolines. Cold, sunny locations such as the Pyrenees are most promising for solar viability.

SOLAR SYSTEMS

- Elements
- Modes
- Design Tools

Elements

This chapter discusses the five basic elements involved in any solar heating system: solar collector, storage, distribution system, auxiliary heater and controls.

INTRODUCTION

To utilize the sun's energy, it must be *collected, stored*, then *distributed* at the appropriate time. This process must be *controlled,* and an *auxiliary heater* provided for the times when there is not sufficient solar energy available or stored to satisfy the heating load. This solar strategy will apply to both domestic hot water systems and swimming pool installations, as well as solar assisted space heating schemes. The discussion below, however, concentrates on space heating systems, though most of the elements discussed are directly applicable to the other two types of systems.

SOLAR COLLECTORS

There are two basic kinds of solar collectors

- *buildings as solar collectors* where a glazed south side of a structure acts as a solar collector, and

- *panels as solar collectors* where an independent piece of solar hardware is attached to the building structure.

The greenhouse effect (12) is employed in both these collector types. Glass has the peculiar property of being transparent to short wavelengths (i.e. solar radiation) but opaque to long wavelengths (as emitted by most earthly objects). Thus heat can be trapped behind glass.

BUILDINGS AS SOLAR COLLECTORS
On a sunny day a room with a large south facing window will become warm (13). Here the building structure acts as an absorber, and the window creates the greenhouse effect.

PANELS AS SOLAR COLLECTORS
These generally consist of a metal plate (the absorber) that is angled towards the sun (14). Solar radiation strikes the plate and it warms up. Heat is prevented from leaving the back by insulation, such as glass fibre, and from the front by a sheet of glass, bringing into play the greenhouse effect. To transport the accumulated heat away, water in tubes or air in ducts is passed from the bottom of the collector to the top (14b, 14c).

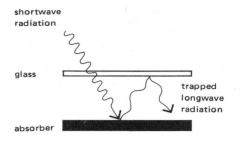
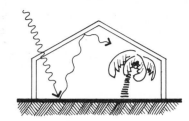

(a) The heated surface emits long wave radiation that is trapped behind the glass.

(b) This principle is applied to heat greenhouses.

12 THE GREENHOUSE EFFECT

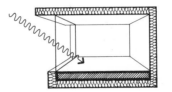
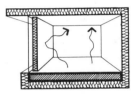

(a) South facing glass permits solar radiation to warm the thermal mass (eg floor).

(b) Insulating shutters prevent the stored heat escaping at night-time.

13 BUILDINGS AS SOLAR COLLECTORS

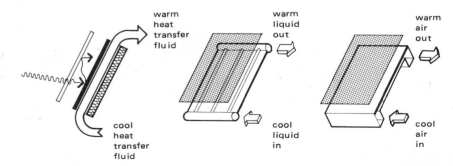

(a) The principle: trapped heat warms the heat transfer fluid

(b) Liquid flat plate collector

(c) Air flat plate collector

14 PANELS AS SOLAR COLLECTORS

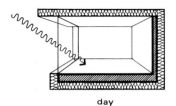
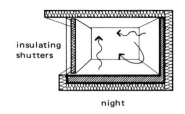

day   night

15 BUILDING FABRIC STORAGE. Heat stored in the day is released at night.

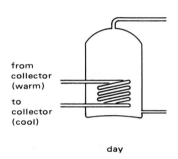
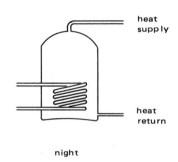

from collector (warm)

to collector (cool)

heat supply

heat return

day   night

16 WATER CYLINDER STORAGE. During the day warm liquid from the collectors heats the storage water. At night, the warm storage water is distributed to the building.

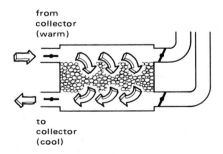
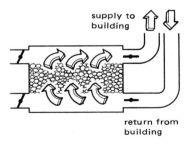

from collector (warm)

to collector (cool)

supply to building

return from building

day   night

17 ROCK BIN STORAGE. During the day warm air from the collector heats the rocks. At night, cool room air is heated by the warm rocks.

STORAGE

The heat collected from the sun in space heating schemes is generally stored in the building fabric itself, water filled cylinders or large containers filled with fist sized rocks, called rock bins.

BUILDING FABRIC STORAGE

When the sun has set on a summer's day, brick walls and concrete pavements are still warm, having soaked up the heat of the day (storing it), with the ability to release heat for some time afterwards (thus distributing it).

In solar buildings **(15)** brick walls, concrete floors, etc store heat energy during the day by being exposed to the sun's radiation, releasing it to the cool room at night. Insulating shutters keep night-time heat losses to a minimum.

WATER CYLINDER STORAGE

Long after turning off the power, the water remaining in a kettle is still warm. Water has an excellent heat storing capacity (it can store about twice as much heat as concrete or brickwork per unit volume).

In solar systems **(16)** warm liquid from liquid flat plate collectors heats water stored in metal cylinders, usually made of copper. When required the warm storage water is circulated to the building's heating system.

ROCK BIN STORAGE

Hot air blown through cool rocks will heat the rocks and cool the air. Conversely, cool air blown through warm rocks will heat the air and cool the rocks.

In solar systems **(17)** warm air from air flat plate collectors heats the rocks in the rock bin during the day. When required, cool room air is passed through the warm rocks in the opposite direction to heat the air up. Phase change material in containers or water in bottles is sometimes substituted for the fist sized rocks.

Elements

DISTRIBUTION SYSTEMS

Each heat storage medium has its own preferred way of distributing its stored heat.

BUILDING FABRIC STORAGE (18a): The heat stored in the building fabric is transferred directly to the living space by means of radiation, convection and conduction.

WATER CYLINDER STORAGE (18b): The heat stored in the water cylinder (normally located outside the living space) is transferred into the living space by water circulating to fan convectors, panel radiators or underfloor coils.

ROCK BIN STORAGE (18c): The heat stored in the rocks contained in the bin (again normally located outside the living space) is transferred into the living space by air ducted from the rock bin to the living space.

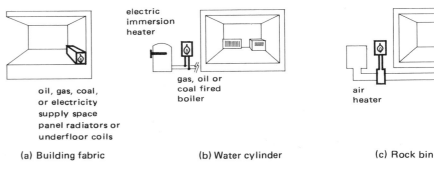

(a) Building fabric storage

(b) Water cylinder storage

(c) Rock bin storage

18 DISTRIBUTION SYSTEMS

AUXILIARY HEATING

Auxiliary heating is necessary not only for extended cloudy periods but also for normal operation. Each heat storage medium has its own preferred auxiliary heating system.

BUILDING FABRIC STORAGE (19a): Virtually any back up system can be used since it is not coupled directly into the solar system; oil, gas, coal or electricity can supply space heaters, panel radiators, underfloor coils etc.

WATER CYLINDER STORAGE (19b): Auxiliary heat can be added into the distribution circuit by boiler (gas, oil or coal fired) or added directly into the water storage cylinder by an electric immersion heater.

ROCK BIN STORAGE (19c): Auxiliary heat is usually added to the supply air stream by incorporating an air heater of some type.

(a) Building fabric

(b) Water cylinder

(c) Rock bin

19 AUXILIARY HEATING

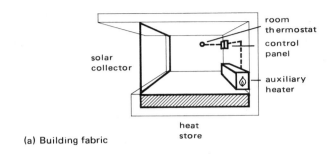

(a) Building fabric

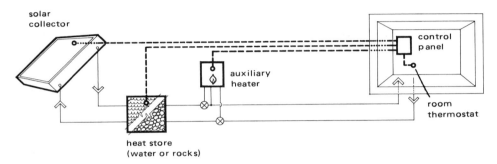

(b) Water and Rock systems

20 CONTROLS

CONTROLS

All heating systems require controls.

In traditional heating systems, a room thermostat is normally the only control, and when the air temperature in the room is too low, the heating is turned on.

In solar systems **(20)**, the temperature in the solar collector and the storage medium is also monitored, so that heat can be efficiently transferred between the solar collector, the heat store and the room in any one of three ways, depending on the temperature in each. These three ways are: from the solar collector to the room direct; from the heat store to the room; and from the solar collector to the heat store. If there is insufficient heat in either the solar collector or the heat store, the auxiliary heating system is switched on.

Most solar control panels are about the size of a brick, and are usually wall mounted. The sensors in the solar collector and the heat store are small (typically 30 mm long and 3 mm diameter) and connected back to the control panel by three- or four-core cable.

21 Elements typically involved when the building acts as a solar collector in a solar assisted space heating scheme. The five basic elements are all present. The large south facing glazing acts as a *solar collector,* with masonry floor and walls acting as the *heat storage medium.* Heat is *distributed* to the living space by radiation, convection and conduction. The room thermostat *controls* the *auxiliary heating* system which in this case is an underfloor heating system.

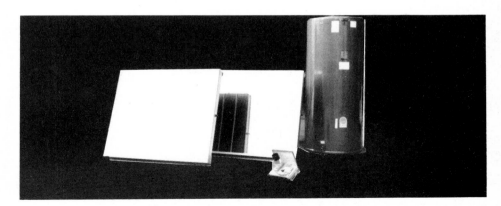

22 Elements typically involved when panels are used as solar collectors in a solar assisted space heating scheme. The five basic elements are provided: (a) *solar collectors;* (b) *heat storage* (here shown as water held in metal containers); (c) *auxiliary heater;* (d) *distribution system;* and (e) *control panel.* The operation of such a system is discussed in the next Chapter.

Modes

This chapter introduces the two basic approaches to solar system design (passive and active) and then examines in detail each of the ten different heating modes available within these two broad approaches.

INTRODUCTION

One of the elementary aims of the building designer is to provide an internal environment that is perceived by the occupants as being thermally comfortable. The climatic factors affecting this comfort level are only four in number; air temperature, air speed, humidity level and solar radiation level. By altering one or any of these four factors the building designer is striving to achieve an environment that lies within the comfort zone, as defined by the comfort zone diagram **(23)**.

The *solar* building designer is no different. By using the five *elements* discussed in the last chapter, he also strives to achieve an environment that lies within the comfort zone. Those *elements* at his disposal can be arranged in many ways, but generally such arrangements fall into two broad approaches, passive and active. Each of these approaches is conveniently made up of five different heating modes.

These heating modes have been specifically categorised for space heating schemes. The more familiar solar applications of domestic hot water systems and swimming pool schemes generally fall under the heading of liquid flat plate collectors, but it is best to refer to specialist books dealing exclusively with these two topics (see the Bibliography) rather than attempt to force the peculiar traits of these systems onto this space heating classification. In passing it should be noted, however, that domestic hot water schemes are usually incorporated into liquid flat plate collector systems because of the similarity of the two.

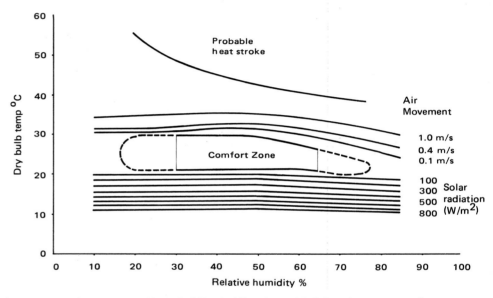

(source: Koeningsberger et al, *Manual of Tropical Housing and Buildings,* Longman 1973)

23 COMFORT ZONE DIAGRAM

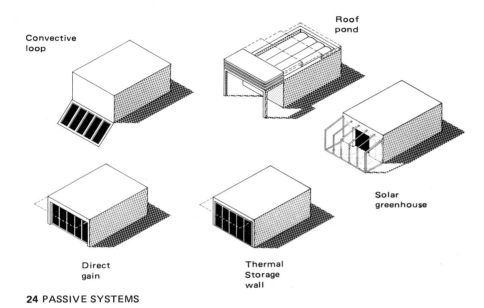

Convective loop

Roof pond

Solar greenhouse

Direct gain

Thermal Storage wall

24 PASSIVE SYSTEMS

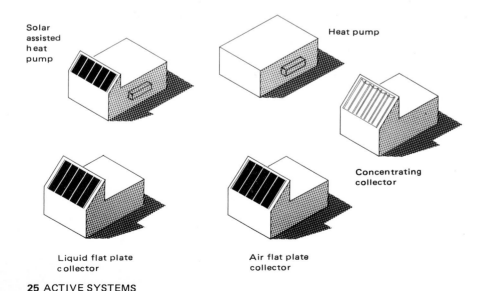

Solar assisted heat pump

Heat pump

Concentrating collector

Liquid flat plate collector

Air flat plate collector

25 ACTIVE SYSTEMS

PASSIVE SYSTEMS:

Passive systems can be defined as those where the control of the flow of thermal energy is by natural means.

Generally, these systems use the building as the collector.

Below are the five generic types of passive heating systems **(24)** that are described in more detail on the following pages.

(1)   Direct gain

(2)   Thermal storage wall

(3)   Solar greenhouse

(4)   Roof pond

(5)   Convective loop.

ACTIVE SYSTEMS

Active systems can be defined as those where external energy (usually electricity) is used to pump water or blow air from the solar collector to a separate store or living space, in order to transfer the heat from one place to the other.

Below are the five generic types of active heating systems **(25)** described in more detail on later pages.

(1)   Liquid flat plate collector

(2)   Air flat plate collector

(3)   Concentrating collector

(4)   Heat pump

(5)   Solar assisted heat pump.

Passive and active solar systems are not mutually exclusive; the application of one or the other will depend entirely on the project under consideration. The ten heating modes should be seen as the overall range of solar design tools available to the building designer. Most buildings will benefit from the incorporation of either one or the other approach, or alternatively, a combination of both. Such combinations are sometimes referred to in solar literature as **hybrids**.

Modes

DIRECT GAIN

A large expanse of vertical south facing glass **(26)** usually double glazed admits the sun's rays, allowing them to strike the masonry floor and/or walls which act as thermal storage. The thermal energy stored in these elements is distributed to the living space by radiation, by convection of room air over the warm surfaces and by conduction. A correctly designed mass can contain internal temperature swings to 10°C.

The system can be controlled in many ways: movable insulated shutters used at night can reduce heat loss; external reflectors can increase solar gain; external blinds and overhangs can reduce overheating; and vertical glazing will allow the low winter sun to penetrate at nearly right angles, whilst reflecting the high, glancing rays of the summer sun. An English example of this passive heating mode is the Wallasey School, Cheshire.

THERMAL STORAGE WALL

This heating mode **(27)** blocks and collects solar radiation outside the living space by creating a thermally massive wall between it and the sun. Heat is stored in this thermal mass and distributed to the living space by re-radiation through the back of the wall, and/or by convection of cool room air past the warm face of the mass by natural thermosyphoning. This thermosyphoning effect is created on the sunny face of the wall by placing a glazed screen about 50 mm away from the wall face, punching holes in the top and bottom of the wall, and letting room air naturally thermosyphon and become warm. Such walls are known as *Trombe walls*. When horizontally stacked drums of water are used for the thermal mass, it is known as a *drum wall*, and when vertical tubes of water are substituted it is known as a *water wall*.

Control of this heating mode is effected in several ways: the size of the thermal mass is optimised to ensure a sufficient time lag before re-radiation occurs; external blinds and overhangs reduce summer overheating; and manually operated dampers can control the direction and volume of thermosyphoning air. An English example of this passive heating mode is the Higher Bebington development, Cheshire.

SOLAR GREENHOUSE

The heating mode **(28)** is a development of the *Trombe wall*, but the space between the glass and the wall has been widened to form a greenhouse. The thermal movements are very similar, as are the controls. The greenhouse, however, provides not only a means of heating but also a usable living space and the opportunity to grow food and flowers. An English example of this passive heating mode is The Horse and Gate house, Cambridgeshire.

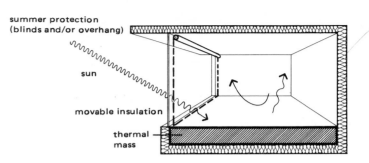

26 DIRECT GAIN: Shortwave radiation from the sun enters the living space and strikes the thermal mass. Heat is distributed from this mass by longwave radiation (which cannot pass through glass), by convection of room air over the slab, and by conduction (if one sits or stands on the thermal mass). Movable insulation keeps the heat in at night.

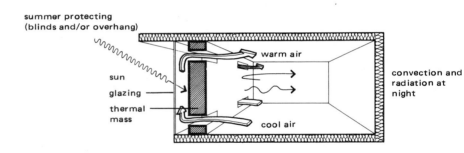

27 THERMAL STORAGE WALLS: Shortwave radiation from the sun strikes the thermal mass. During a winter's day cool room air cycles up between the glass and the warmed mass, re-entering the room space at the top. During a winter's night, heat that has diffused through the wall is radiated to the living space, while room air is also heated by convection.

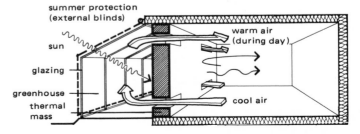

28 SOLAR GREENHOUSE: The thermal movements are similar to the movements in the *thermal storage wall* above, but the space between the glass and the wall has been widened to form a greenhouse.

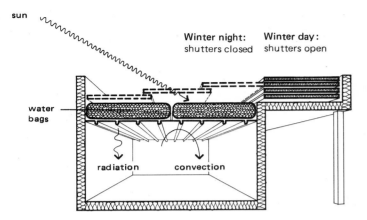

29 ROOF POND: During a winter's day, shortwave radiation from the sun strikes the water. The room is heated by radiation and convection. At night the heat stored by the water is conserved by closing the shutters and the room is still heated by radiation and convection. The system is not particularly suitable for northern European climates.

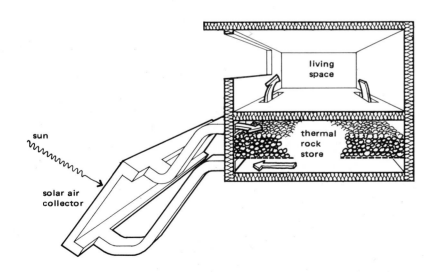

30 CONVECTIVE LOOP: During a winter's day, air is heated by the collector and naturally thermocycles through the rock store where it loses its heat, returning to the base of the collector. The living space is heated by thermocycling warm air from the store into the room.

ROOF POND

This heating mode **(29)** transfers the thermal storage to the roof, and consists of plastic bags of water that are supported on a steel deck roof.

Control is effected by the positioning of movable insulating shutters that are located above the water bags. In the winter mode, the insulation covers are left open during the day to allow the radiation to be absorbed and re-radiated into the living space, whilst at night the covers are closed to conserve heat. In the summer mode, the covers are left open at night to take advantage of the night-time radiation and convection, whilst during the day the covers are closed to protect the bags from heat input, allowing the cool water to absorb heat from the living space.

The movable insulation panels can be automatically opened and closed depending on the indoor temperature, the storage water temperature and the sol-air temperature.

There are no examples of this heating mode in Britain, and it is really not suited to northern climates where low winter sun angles make horizontal collection inefficient, and the relatively mild summers make its cooling potential somewhat unnecessary.

CONVECTIVE LOOP

In this system **(30)** an angled solar collector heats a transport fluid (that can be either air or water) and, by a thermosyphoning loop, allows it to rise to a thermal store located above the collector. After transferring its heat to the store, the fluid continues down to re-enter the base of the collector.

Control is effected first by the correct sizing of the thermal store and collector and second by the use of dampers to regulate the direction and volume of air moving between the collector, the rock store and the living space.

There are no examples of this space heating mode in Britain, but a significant proportion of domestic solar hot water heaters use this principle.

Modes

LIQUID FLAT PLATE COLLECTOR

In this heating mode (31) liquid (usually water) is used to transfer heat in two circuits. In the primary circuit, the sun's radiation heats up the liquid in the collector, which is then pumped to the thermal store. Here it dumps its heat via a heat exchanger. In the secondary circuit, heat is picked up from the thermal store (either directly by use of the thermal store water, or indirectly by use of a heat exchanger) and pumped to a distribution component (e.g. a fan convector unit as shown or oversized panel radiators, or underfloor tubes). Auxiliary heat can be provided by a fossil fuel boiler connected into this secondary circuit, or by an electric immersion heater located in the thermal store itself. An English example of this active heating mode is the Milton Keynes house.

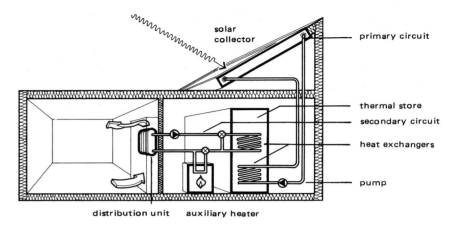

31 LIQUID FLAT PLATE COLLECTOR

AIR FLAT PLATE COLLECTOR

This system (32) is essentially the same as the liquid system above, but here *air instead of water* is used to transfer heat in the two circuits. These two circuits can be either separated or combined.

In the first circuit of a typical installation the sun's radiation heats up the air in the collector which is then blown to the thermal rock store. If dampers a and b are closed, it is then forced down through the rocks, giving up its heat. Fan d then extracts it for another heating cycle. In the second circuit, with fan d turned off and damper c closed, room air is extracted by fan e, forced up through the rock store, where it collects heat, and passed back into the room. Auxiliary heat can be supplied on this circuit. The rock store alone, or both the rock store and collector, can be bypassed if insufficient heat is available. An English example of this heating mode is the Kippford house, though its heat storage and distribution system differs from the one cited above.

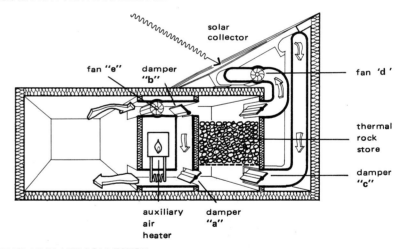

32 AIR FLAT PLATE COLLECTOR

CONCENTRATING COLLECTORS

This system (33) is the same as the liquid flat plate collector system, except that the flat plate collectors are replaced by an array of concentrating collectors. These dished collectors concentrate the sun's radiation onto the liquid carrying pipes.

These collectors are far more suitable to climates with plentiful direct radiation, rather than our cloudy, intermittent weather. There are no British examples.

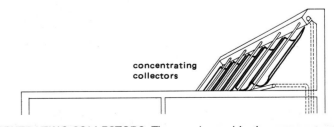

33 CONCENTRATING COLLECTORS. They can be used in the same way as the liquid flat plate collector system, except that the flat plate collectors are replaced by concentrating collectors.

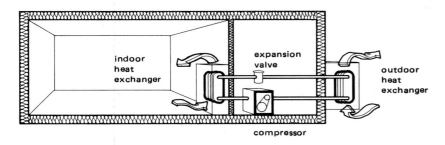

34 HEAT PUMP

HEAT PUMP

This active heating mode **(34)** is somewhat different to the preceding modes. It makes use of solar energy that has already been collected and stored outdoors in the air, the ground and bodies of water. By means of a small machine (acting like an airconditioner in reverse) it transfers this heat from outside to inside. This machine is usually powered by an electric motor that will produce about 3 kWh of heat for every 1 kWh of electricity consumed, the 2 kWh difference being the heat extracted from the air, the ground or the body of water.

In a typical machine that uses air as the heat source, and air as the internal heating medium (known as an air/air machine), outside air is blown over the outdoor heat exchanger thus heating a volatile liquid inside and causing it to evaporate. The resulting vapour is compressed and becomes hotter (like the air in a bicycle pump after inflating a tyre) and is forced inside by the compressor. Cool room air is blown over the indoor heat exchanger causing the hot vapour to condense (like hot breath on cold glass) and release its heat to the heat exchanger and thus to the room air passing over it. The condensed liquid (still at high pressure) is then forced through the expansion valve where it drops in pressure and becomes cooler, ready for the next cycle.

There are thousands of heat pumps in operation in Britain.

SOLAR ASSISTED HEAT PUMP

Heat pumps can be used in conjunction with conventional flat plate collector solar heating systems **(35)**. It is possible to integrate the heat pump in three ways.

- *in parallel* where the heat pump using outside air acts as an auxiliary heat source. Direct solar heating is used whenever possible, with the heat pump operating whenever there is insufficient solar energy.

- *in series* where the heat pump is located between the solar system and the space heating load. The heat pump uses solar heated water as its heat source.

- *dual source* where the heat pump is arranged so that it can use both outside air and solar heated water as its sources of heat.

It is still unclear if these combinations will offer substantial savings when compared with totally separate heat pump or solar systems.

Diagram **(35)** illustrates a dual source system.

There are no British examples that fall ideally into this category, but two examples use solar preheated air as their heat sources: the Wilson house and the Livingston house.

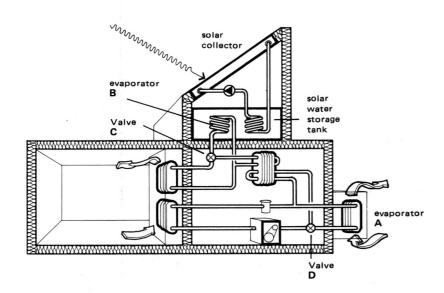

35 SOLAR ASSISTED HEAT PUMP: dual source. Heat may be extracted either from outdoor air via evaporator **A** or from solar heated water via evaporator **B**. Valves **C** and **D** determine which heat source shall be used. Heat is distributed to the living space via the heater exchanger.

Design Tools

This chapter presents a series of design tools to assist with the integration of solar energy technology into buildings. They are listed in order of scale rather than importance.

INTRODUCTION

These design tools represent the wide variety of approaches available to the building designer. With experience, they will become familiar words in a design language, to be applied at the appropriate time and in the appropriate situation. The sizes given are approximate only, and thus represent only a reasonable starting point. Final sizing must be done by the solar engineer.

The extent and scope of these design tools are not exhaustive, but the intention is to cover the major areas of concern. The bias is towards small scale housing, but the principles demonstrated will hold for most scales and types of building. The detail of the points discussed has been kept to a minimum for clarity and appreciation, and the development of these ideas with all their involved subtleties and calculation procedures may be carried out later, in consultation with the solar engineer or by reference to specialist books on each topic (see References).

The case for energy conservation is difficult to overstate. Huge inroads into the amount of energy used by a building can be made by careful use of traditional formats: insulation, weather-stripping, double glazing etc. It is only after these measures are taken that the method of heating (be it solar-assisted or conventional) should be considered.

This chapter is divided into two sections, each section having three sub-sections:

SITE PLANNING:	Energy Conservation
	Passive Space Heating Modes
	Active Space Heating Modes
BUILDING PLANNING:	Energy Conservation
	Passive Space Heating Modes
	Active Space Heating Modes

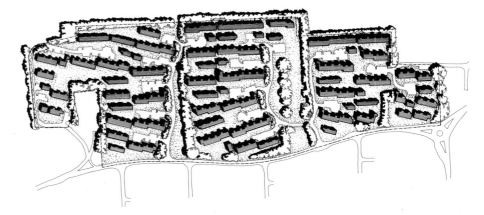

36 Site plan of Northlands 1 Housing at Basildon, Essex, that demonstrates most of the principles discussed on the next page.

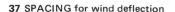

37 SPACING for wind deflection

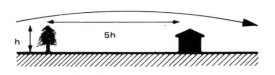

38 BERMING for added insulation and wind deflection

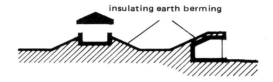

insulating earth berming

39 GLAZING to maximise solar gain and reduce heat losses.

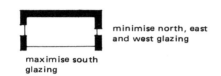

maximise south glazing

minimise north, east and west glazing

40 BUILDING SHAPE to maximise solar gain possibilities and reduce heat losses.

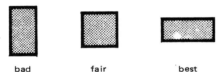

bad   fair   best

41 ORIENTATION to maximise solar possibilities

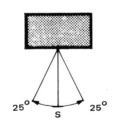

25°   25°
S

42 SPACING to reduce overshadowing

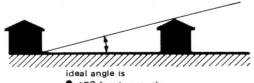

ideal angle is
● 15° for due south obstruction
● 10° for any other obstructions

SITE PLANNING

ENERGY CONSERVATION

● use vegetation to deflect heat robbing winds **(37)** that in the UK mostly come from the north-east. Her Majesty's Stationery Office produces several publications on wind speeds and directions.

● use vegetation to provide shade in summer.

● allow winds to circulate for summer cooling that in the UK generally come from the south-west.

● use earth berming (earth banked against the side of a building) and earth roofing to add insulation to the building and help deflect winds **(38).**

PASSIVE SPACE HEATING MODES

● maximise south facing glazing to maximise solar gain **(39)**, aiming to achieve an unshaded window from 9 a.m. to 3 p.m. every day of the year. Ensure protection for summer overheating.

● use the most appropriate building shape **(40)** to reduce heat losses and maximise solar gain potential.

● use the most appropriate building orientation **(41)** to maximise solar possibilities. Buildings facing within 45° of south can benefit from solar heating, but it is preferable to limit the deviation to within 25° of south.

● use the most appropriate spacing **(42)** between buildings to maximise solar potential by minimising collector overshadowing. In southern Britain, solar radiation intensities below a 10° altitude angle are negligible, so obstructions in any direction below 10° are not important. However, due south obstructions should not preclude noon sunlight on the midwinter's day (providing of course there is any). The altitude angle at this time of the year in London is 15°.

ACTIVE SPACE HEATING MODES

● use a site layout that will maximise the solar potential (by correct orientation) and will minimise the overshadowing of any roof mounted solar collector. The same principles applied in the Passive Space Heating Modes section above will apply here, except that the reference point for measuring the altitude of the sun will normally be at roof level, rather than at ground level. This will usually permit buildings to be placed closer together.

Design Tools

BUILDING PLANNING

ENERGY CONSERVATION

(a) Insulation

- insulate the building fabric well, to the highest degree possible. (Walls 0.4 $W/m^2{}^oC$ or less; roof 0.35 $W/m^2{}^oC$ or less). Provide underfloor insulation, at least to the perimeter.

- check that condensation will not occur (refer to Burberry, P. *Building for Energy Conservation*, p. 28–30 for detail).

- eliminate cold bridges, i.e. sections of the building structure that connect the warm inside to the cold outside, which elsewhere are separated by insulation.

- provide a vapour barrier between the insulation and the room space.

- double glaze major window areas (double glazing takes approximately twenty years to be cost effective, but it is now socially accepted and increases the mean radiant temperature of the otherwise "cold" window).

- use movable insulation for *all* windows.

- consider earth berming and earth roofing to increase insulation levels.

(b) Ventilation

- reduce air infiltration. Normal building construction has about 1½ to 2 air changes per hour. This can be reduced to below 1: by caulking up window and door frames in the building structure; by providing weatherseals to all openings (i.e. doors, window sashes, letter box holes etc.); by providing dampers to chimneys; and by sealing gaps between major elements (i.e. the gap between floors and walls at skirting level)

- provide a controlled ventilation system that is fitted with a heat exchanger that transfers heat from warm stale expelled air to cold fresh incoming air.

- protect entries by locating on leeward side. Use draught lobbies.

- provide separate utility room with exhaust to outside, in order to reduce the level of unwanted moisture in the air.

- consider using stair as cooling shaft in summer by providing roof level opening.

(c) Temperature Zoning

- group rooms with like temperatures together (i.e. living and dining at say 21^oC; bedrooms, stairs and utility room at say 15^oC).

- group rooms that need to be warmer on the south, and those that can be cooler on the north. Place unheated rooms (e.g. storage) on the north.

- control unwanted heat flow between levels by avoiding double height volumes. Enclose stairs and provide with access doors at top or bottom.

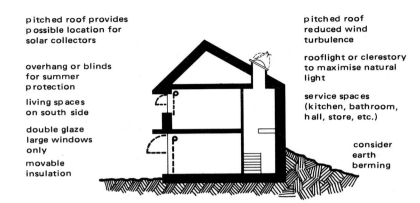

pitched roof provides possible location for solar collectors

overhang or blinds for summer protection

living spaces on south side

double glaze large windows only

movable insulation

pitched roof reduced wind turbulence

rooflight or clerestory to maximise natural light

service spaces (kitchen, bathroom, hall, store, etc.)

consider earth berming

43 TYPICAL SECTION showing energy conservation features.

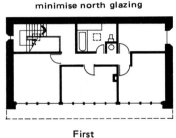

minimise north glazing

provide stair with door to prevent heat rising uncontrolled to first floor

reduce east and west glazing

insulate building fabric well

First Floor

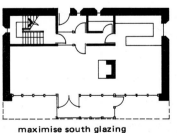

provide protected entry

locate service space on north side

locate living space on south side

group warmer rooms together on ground floor

provide separate utility room with exhaust to reduce unwanted moisture in air

centrally locate all heat producing equipment (boilers, fireplaces, h.w.s.) so heat losses benefit building

maximise south glazing (provide summer protection)

Ground Floor

44 TYPICAL PLANS showing energy conservation features.

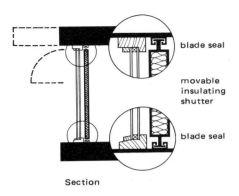
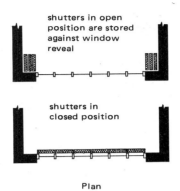

Section

Plan

45 Movable insulation for windows

46 Photograph of shutters described above (by courtesey of Insulated Window Shutters Ltd, Huddersfield).

(d) Windows

- select window locations judiciously. Minimise north facing, reduce east and west facing, and maximise south facing, provided that they are protected by overhangs or external blinds for summer control.
- provide movable insulated shutters or blinds to all windows. Allow sufficient window reveal to accept these blinds or shutters.
- double glaze only major window areas to reduce the "cold panel" effect.

(e) Lighting

- locate tasks requiring greatest illumination near windows.
- consider high clerestories or rooflights to maximise natural lighting.

(f) Building Volume/Shape

- reduce the surface area that surrounds the building volume to a minimum.
- if projections are necessary, it is preferable if they are unheated spaces.
- use pitched roof shapes to reduce wind turbulence and also provide possible locations for solar collectors.
- reduce the internal volume that has to be heated.

(g) Colour

- if the building fabric *is* heavily insulated, the external colour will make little thermal difference.
- if for some unavoidable reason the building fabric *is not* heavily insulated, the south facades should be dark, the east and west light and the north any colour.
- use dark colours internally for materials that are *used* for heat storage (e.g. brick walls, concrete floors).
- use light colours internally for materials that are *not used* for heat storage.
- use light colours internally to increase the level of natural illumination.

(h) Domestic Hot Water

- in all new buildings, provide solar preheating. Consider the use of a third tap, a *solar tap*, that draws water directly from the preheat tank to provide lukewarm water, instead of mixing hot and cold.
- centrally locate h.w.s. and provide at least 100 mm of insulation.
- insulate all hot water pipes.
- provide showers as well as baths, since energy savings of up to 35% are possible. Consider using spray taps to reduce water consumption.
- consider recovering the heat lost in waste water by incorporating a water/water heat exchanger.

Design Tools

BUILDING PLANNING

PASSIVE SPACE HEATING MODES

General

- concentrate glazing on south side.
- allow approximately 40—50% of floor area for passive collector area in domestic situations.
- orientate passive collector due south, $\pm\ 25^{O}$.
- provide movable insulation behind passive collector glazing.
- provide reflective shutters to increase solar radiation collection (increases of up to 30% are possible).
- provide correct shading for summer.
- allow for cross ventilation for summer cooling.

(1) Direct Gain

- double glaze main collector area.
- consider using diffuse glass to reduce glare.
- allow movable insulation to be so located on cold, cloudy winter days that only the minimum glazed area required for natural illumination is uninsulated, the remainder of the window being insulated.
- for clerestorey collection, make plan width (w) approximately 1 to 1.5 the floor/ceiling height (h). **(48b).**
- for sawtooth configuration, make pitch equal to winter solstice altitude (London 15°, Edinburgh 11°). **(48c).**

(2) Thermal Storage Wall

- single glazing in front of thermal mass.
- provide thermal mass by using
  (a) masonry (approximately 300—450 mm thick): *Trombe wall* **(49a)**
  (b) water tubes (say 300 mm diameter and room height): *Water wall* **(49b)**
  (c) water drums (perhaps 55 gallon drums laid on their side): *Drum wall* **(49c).**

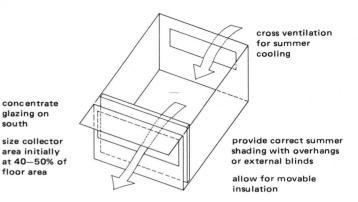

concentrate glazing on south

size collector area initially at 40—50% of floor area

cross ventilation for summer cooling

provide correct summer shading with overhangs or external blinds

allow for movable insulation

47 GENERAL PRINCIPLES

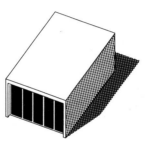 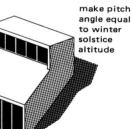 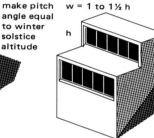

make pitch angle equal to winter solstice altitude

w = 1 to 1½ h

(a) one room depth using main window exclusively

(b) two room depth using clerestory and main window

(c) multiple room depth using clerestory exclusively

48 DIRECT GAIN

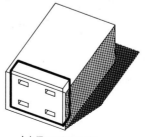 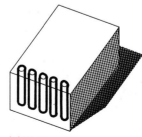 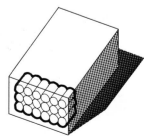

(a) Trombe wall: vertical masonry wall

(b) Water wall; vertical tubes of water

(c) Drum wall: horizontal drums of water

49 THERMAL STORAGE WALL

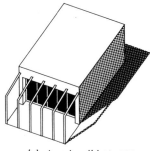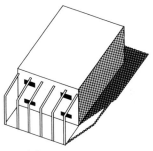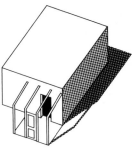

(a) glazed wall between greenhouse and living space

(b) Massive wall between greenhouse and living space

(c) small greenhouse used as entry porch

50 SOLAR GREENHOUSE

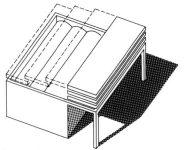

51 ROOF POND: not an appropriate heating mode in northern Europe.

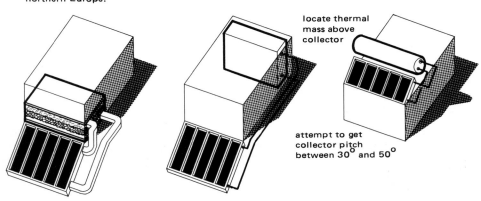

locate thermal mass above collector

attempt to get collector pitch between 30° and 50°

(a) Air space heating system

(b) liquid space heating system

(c) Roof mounted collector for domestic hot water system

52 CONVECTIVE LOOP

(3) Solar Greenhouse

- depending on the use of the greenhouse, locate movable insulation directly behind the glass, or between the greenhouse and the living space.
- the wall between the greenhouse and the living space can be either solid or glazed **(50a** and **50b).**
- mechanically extract overheated air to a separate insulated storage for use later on.
- consider plants and earth in the greenhouse as thermal mass.
- use the greenhouse as an entry porch if appropriate **(50c).**

(4) Roof Pond

- an inappropriate heating mode for northern European climates because of its high thermal mass, its requirement for solar radiation at relatively normal angles of incidence, its unwanted ability to achieve summer cooling to clear night skies and its untraditional European building form.

(5) Convective Loop

- slope collector as appropriate (begin at 45°). (For discussion of collector slopes see next page).
- locate thermal storage above collector **(52).**

Design Tools

BUILDING PLANNING

ACTIVE SPACE HEATING MODES

General

- the orientation of the collectors (53a) should preferably be within 25° of south, but to be within 40° is acceptable.
- the pitch of the collectors (53b) should preferably be within 30° and 50°, but pitches between 20° to 30° and 50° to 70° are acceptable.
- in Britain, a useful starting point for collector sizing in domestic situations is to allow 40—50% of the floor area. More accurate sizing will be calculated by the solar engineer as the building design proceeds.
- the location of the collector is best if it receives unobstructed solar radiation from 9 a.m. to 3 p.m. every day of the year.

(1) Liquid flat plate collector (54)

- locate collectors for maximum solar radiation availability.
- provide thermal storage, initially sized between 50 and 100 litres per m² of collector for a water cylinder storage system.
- allow for insulated pipes to connect collector and thermal storage, say one supply and one return, 75 mm diameter each.
- allow for auxiliary boiler, control panel and distribute heat by fan convector, panel radiators or underfloor coils.
- provide easy access for glass replacement and system maintenance.
- have structural engineer allow for dead weight and wind loading of collectors.

(2) Air flat plate collector (55)

- locate collectors for maximum solar radiation availability.
- provide thermal storage, initially sized between 0.1 and 0.3 m³ per m² of collector for rock bin storage system.
- allow for insulated ducts to connect collector and thermal storage, say one supply and one return, and each, say, 600 mm by 300 mm.
- allow for auxiliary air heater, control panel and distribute heat via forced air system.
- provide easy access for glass replacement and system maintenance.
- have structural engineer allow for dead weight and wind loading of collectors.

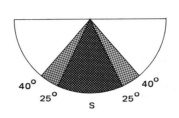

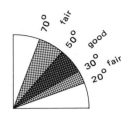

size collector area initially at 40—50% of floor area

(a) collector orientation

(b) collector pitch

(c) collector area

53 GENERAL PRINCIPLES

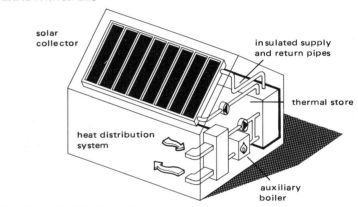

solar collector

insulated supply and return pipes

thermal store

heat distribution system

auxiliary boiler

54 LIQUID FLAT PLATE COLLECTOR

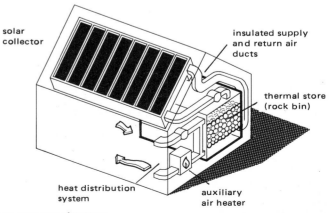

solar collector

insulated supply and return air ducts

thermal store (rock bin)

heat distribution system

auxiliary air heater

55 AIR FLAT PLATE COLLECTOR

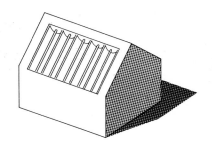

56 CONCENTRATING COLLECTORS: not an
appropriate heating mode in northern Europe.

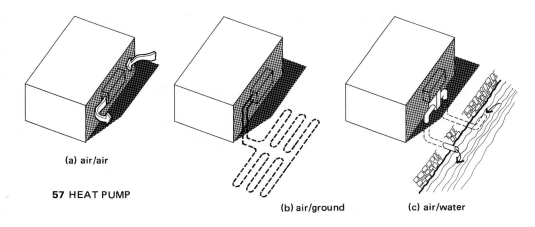

(a) air/air

57 HEAT PUMP

(b) air/ground   (c) air/water

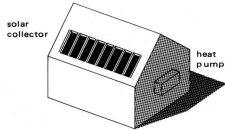

solar
collector

heat
pump

58 SOLAR ASSISTED HEAT PUMP

(3) Concentrating collectors **(56)**

- an inappropriate heating mode for northern European climates because the system really requires an approximate daily average of 6–8 hours of direct sunshine to be economical.

(4) Heat pump

- heat pump installations are independent of the building's orientation.
- heat pump installations can draw heat from the air **(57a)**, the earth **(57b)** or bodies of water **(57c).**
- initially provide a space 1.200 metre cube for the heat pump machine in domestic applications.
- sound isolate the heat pump machine from the rest of the building.
- distribute heat from heat pump by ducted air **(57),** underfloor coils, fan convectors or panel radiators.

(5) Solar assisted heat pump **(58)**

- the locating of the heat pump is independent of the building's orientation.
- the locating of the solar collectors used in conjunction with the heat pump is limited to the same conditions as conventional air or liquid flat plate systems, described in *(1)* and *(2)* above.
- for domestic installations, initially allow 25% of the floor area for solar collector area, and a 1.200 metre cube for the heat pump installation.
- distribute heat by ducted air, underfloor coils, fan convectors or panel radiators.

IMPLEMENTATION

- Plan of Work
- Authorities

Plan of Work

This chapter describes an outline plan of work that can be followed to achieve a building that has solar assisted space and/or water heating.

INTRODUCTION

Once the decision is made to examine the possibility of utilizing solar energy for a building project the traditional building team process can be followed. It is only varied by:

(a) the designer becoming more acutely aware of the possibilities of orientation, windows, insulation etc. (described in Chapters 3, 4 and 5).

(b) employing a solar engineer instead of a heating and ventilating engineer (a list of some of the practising British solar engineers is given in Appendix C).

The following plan of work is based on the Royal Institute of British Architects "Outline Plan of Work" 1973.

BRIEFING

Inception:
*   Client organisation set up for briefing. Requirements considered and architect appointed.

Feasibility:
*   Initial feasibility of project carried out, studying user requirements, design and cost restraints, site conditions including weather and sun data, and building type and pattern of occupation (important in selecting solar system). Written brief prepared. (Climatic data sources are noted in Chapter 2 and Appendix B, but the solar engineer should be consulted at the earliest possible time to advise on what solar information is required and where and how it should be obtained.)

Consultants:
*   Consultants appointed as necessary including solar engineer (a list of some of the practising British solar engineers is given in Appendix C).

SKETCH PLAN

Outline proposals
*   Initial planning exercise involving all consultants carried out. Rules of Thumb (see Chapter 5) used to size elements of the selected solar system (see Chapter 3) in consultation with solar engineer.
*   Materials used in building fabric selected to provide the appropriate U-value and correct thermal capacity for a lightweight or heavyweight building, in consulation with the solar engineer. In general, though, thermally lightweight buildings have a *quick thermal response* (i.e. take a short time to heat up and a short time to cool down after the heating source is removed, be it the sun, the occupants, lights or the heating system) and are suitable for buildings that have intermittent occupation patterns (i.e. student housing). Thermally heavyweight buildings, however, have a *slow thermal response* (i.e. take a long time to heat up but remain warm after the heating source is removed) and are suitable for buildings that have a continuous occupation pattern (i.e. elderly people's homes).

Scheme design
*   Final sketch plan prepared that leaves room for manoeuvring at a later date (including manoeuvres in the solar system).
*   Thermal analysis of building prepared by the solar engineer after the design is finalised in preparation for next design stage.

Cost check
*   Building cost checked in traditional manner, incorporating solar elements costed and evaluated by the solar engineer in conjunction with the Quantity Surveyor.

Approval
*   Initial discussion held with all authorities (see Chapter 7).

WORKING DRAWINGS

Documents
*   Prepare working documents and specifications in traditional manner incorporating solar elements inconsultation with solar engineer.
*   Prepare Bill of Quantities (if required) in traditional manner incorporating solar elements in consultation with solar engineer. Contingency sums for both the building and solar system to be included and a sum allocated for the commissioning of the solar system, in the same way as a sum is allocated for commissioning a traditional heating system.

Solar engineer to prepare detailed thermal analysis of building and solar system to predict likely performance. This analysis will be based on the working drawings that should be flexible enough to incorporate variations on site to both the building and the solar system (with funds provided for by the Contingency Sums).

Tendering
- Documents put out to tender (solar engineer to handle solar elements if required).
- Contractor appointed.

SITE OPERATIONS

Construction
- Building erected, with solar engineer supervising solar elements of work.

Completion
- Building handed over to client along with traditional building maintenance manual (if required). Solar engineer to prepare and issue to client a maintenance manual for the solar system.

Defects liability period
- Normal maintenance operations for building and solar system seen through one heating season. If possible solar system should be monitored to check that system is performing as expected.
- Adjustments to building and solar system carried out before final hand over.

Feedback
- If agreeable, the occupier to keep records of energy consumption (unless system is automatically monitored) in order to provide solar engineer with feedback data.

Authorities

This chapter discusses the requirements of the various authorities likely to be encountered, and a description of some of the guides pertinent to solar installations in Britain.

INTRODUCTION

In Britain there is no uniformity in the attitude of the authorities to solar installations. Like most architects and non-technical people, they are unfamiliar with solar energy, both in its technology and its application. Solar energy systems, however, are almost entirely made up from materials and techniques familiar to the Authority; their novelty lies only in the manner in which they are assembled. Some regulations are more applicable to active systems than passive systems (since they involve solar panels, pumps, pipework etc.) and vice versa.

THE PLANNING DEPARTMENT

Unless the building is in a conservation area or is a listed architectural or historical building, it is unlikely that specific planning permission for the solar installation will be required. However, check before proceeding and ascertain the Authorities' requirements, and obtain their findings in writing to avoid the possibility of later misunderstanding.

SOLAR PANELS:
If these are involved in the scheme, the visual impact of large areas of glass on the roof may be questioned, as well as the potential problem of reflection.

SOLAR RIGHTS:
This question has received little attention in Britain to date, and it appears at the moment there is little, if any, legal protection to solar rights (i.e. guaranteed access to direct solar radiation). Some states in America have passed Bills based on Water Rights (i.e. guaranteed access to water from a river flowing across several States). The State of New Mexico is probably the world leader at the moment and operates on a first come, first served basis to any collector (both passive and active) that produces more than 7.3 kWh on a clear late December day.

In Britain, the best one can do is to check the zoning of the area to the south to ascertain the maximum building height, and to estimate the likely height of vegetation growth to the south that may exclude direct solar radiation.

THE BUILDING CONTROL DEPARTMENT

In Britain, a building permit will almost certainly be required for a new or retrofitted (fitted to an existing structure) solar installation, be it a passive or an active system. Check with the Building Control Officer to ascertain his complete requirements. Listed below are some of the pertinent points that will have to be considered in a building permit application; it should of course be appreciated that this list is not all inclusive, but it does attempt to cover the major issues.

Materials
- check that all specified materials and components conform to relevant Codes and Standards. For the UK consult The Building Regulations 1976 and the British Standards Institute.
- check that materials in solar panels are capable of withstanding temperatures up to 200°C.
- check that material and construction techniques are weather resistant.

Loadings
- check that the loadings applied on, and by, the solar elements conform to relevant Codes and Standards. For the UK consult The Building Regulations 1976 and British Standards Institute.
- items that should be considered include the following:
  (i) check loading on floor structure by thermal storage walls.
  (ii) check loading on roof structure (solar panels, snow, wind, etc.).
  (iii) check solar panels are adequately fixed to roof structure either directly or via a supporting frame.
  (iv) check loading (both positive and negative) on glass and glazing bars used in solar collectors, and check loading on large areas of south facing glass used in passive heating modes. For UK refer to British Standard Code of Practice CP 152 "Glazing and Fixing of Glass".

Fire
- check that the materials used and methods of construction employed conform to relevant Codes and Standards concerning fire. For the UK consult The Building Regulations 1976.
- items that should be considered include the following:
  (i) check fire resistance of materials used.
  (ii) check fire resistance and spread of flame where roof is punctured by solar panels, or where the roof is punctured by fixings or pipes.
  (iii) check that the use of any plastic is satisfactory.
  (iv) check the fire resistance of large glazed areas.

Safety
- check that the materials used and methods of construction employed conform to the relevant Codes and Standards concerning safety. For the UK consult The Building Regulations 1976, The Health and Safety at Work, etc., Act 1974, and British Standard Code of Practice CP 152 "Glazing and Fixing of Glass".
- items that should be considered include the following:
  - (i) check safety of large area of window
  - (ii) check safety of any glass that dislodges areas from solar panels and falls to ground etc.
  - (iii) check safety of projections, obstructions etc. involved with solar installation.
  - (iv) check that solar panels are protected from direct sunlight until the system is operating, to avoid danger and damage from unwanted overheating.

Thermal Insulation
- check that the building fabric complies with the relevant Codes. For the UK consult The Building Regulations 1976.
- in the UK it is unlikely that if large south facing glazed areas are utilized in passive systems the building will comply with the wording of the Regulations. Two energy calculations will have to be done, one to show the energy use of the preferred design that utilizes movable insulation, and another to show the energy use of a building designed according to the Regulations. If the preferred building uses no more energy than the Regulation designed building, it should be approved by the Building Control Officer. If it is not approved, an appeal can be made to the Department of the Environment (Building Regulation Division) who will make a judgement. The solar engineer will be responsible for these calculations, but excellent information is contained in four booklets obtainable from the Solar Energy Advisory Service of Pilkington Flat Glass Limited (see Appendix B for address): "How Windows Save Energy", "How Windows Save Energy — Technical Appendix", "Thermal Transmission of Windows" and "Windows and the New Thermal Insulation Regulations".

Electrical Installation
- check that the solar installation complies with the relevant electrical Codes and safety regulations. For the UK consult The Regulations for the Electrical Equipment of Building issue of 1976, published by the Institution of Electrical Engineers, as well as any additional requirements of the local supply authority.

THE WATER AUTHORITY

The local Water Authority generally needs to be consulted both about new systems and alterations to existing systems. They will usually require a plumbing layout (normally an axonometric), a list of materials used and the size of the components involved. They will also wish to see that *contamination* is eliminated and *wastage* reduced to a minimum. For the UK consult the British Standard Code of Practice CP 310 : 1965 "Water Supply".

The solar engineer will normally provide all of this information for the Authority. Generally such points will only apply to liquid flat plate collector systems, both for space heating and domestic water heating.

Listed below are some of the points the solar engineer will consider.

Contamination
Care should be exercised to eliminate contamination of potable mains water by:
- *preventing backflow* of contaminated fluid into the mains supply of the building. This can be achieved by designing separate circuits for any such contaminated fluids (i.e. water with anti-freeze used in the primary solar collector circuit) and having the circuits filled with a removable hose.
- *preventing leakage* through any barrier which is intended to separate potable from non-potable water, such as the heat exchanger in the thermal store that divides potable water in the thermal storage from contaminated (non-potable) liquid in the primary solar collector circuit.
- *preventing potable water* from coming into contact with materials and substances which adversely affect its potable quality, i.e. lead.
- *not using toxic anti-freeze additives* in solar heating systems. An alternative is to consider the use of de-ionised or distilled water with inhibitors for a long-life system.

Wastage
Wastage of mains supply should be minimised by:
- *checking potential leakage paths* in the systems.
- *minimising dumping water to waste,* with due regard to systems that are designed to drain down for frost protection.
- *minimising dumping water caused by boiling* in summer.

Safety
Many solar engineers consider it advisable (it is not mandatory in the UK) to fit an *anti-scald thermostatically controlled mixing valve.*

In liquid flat plate collector systems having an integrated domestic hot water system, it may be possible in the height of summer for the water to become exceedingly hot, well above the usual 60°C. (A similar overheating of water can occur in a solid fuel back boiler that is enjoying an excessive draught promoted by high winds around the chimney). If this overheating occurs in a solar system that incorporates an anti-scald device, a valve opens and mixes cold water with the hot water until an acceptable temperature level is reached. Unfortunately such anti-scald devices are quite expensive and have been known to fail in open position, i.e. continuously mixing cold water into the hot water supply. The situation should be discussed with the solar engineer.

Authorities

GUIDE DOCUMENTS

WATER HEATING
The following two publications are primarily concerned with solar heating for domestic hot water systems.

Heating and Ventilating Contractors' Association, **Guide to good practice — Solar heating for domestic hot water,** 16 pp, £2.00.

Basically a consumer guide, it covers in clear, concise language design considerations, solar panels, storage vessels, alternative systems, controls, system protection, pumps, pipework, electrical wiring and equipment, and system filling and commissioning. It also contains a check list that suggests the essential information one should find in an estimate for the supply and installation of a solar heating system.

Solar Trade Association, **Solar Water Heating Code of Practice,** 8 pp, £1.00.

This code is non-technical and sets out the principles that govern the conduct of the members of the Association who manufacture, supply and install solar water heating systems for domestic hot water and swimming pool applications. The code covers advertising, selling, permission and approvals, installation, service and repair, complaints and insurance, as well as appendices on Conciliation and Arbitration.

SPACE HEATING
The following two publications give guidance as to the temperature levels required to be achieved in public and private housing for space heating. They make no specific reference to solar.

Homes for Today and Tomorrow, HMSO, 92 pp., £1.75

Most local authority housing in Britain today is built to the standards set out in this report, more commonly referred to as the Parker Morris standard. For space heating, rooms are required to be heated to a certain standard when the outdoor temperature is -1°C; living rooms (18°C), kitchens and halls (13°C) and if possible bedrooms (18°C). There is no specific guidance for solar installations, only for the maintenance of room temperatures.

The National House Building Council, **Registered House — Builders Handbook: Part II,** pp 148, £1.50.

Most private housing is built to this standard or better, and the Handbook proposes four grades of heating. Again, there is no specific guidance for solar installations, only for the maintenance of room temperatures.

The four grades of heating are summarised below:

(a) *Main room heating:* One appliance sized at 42 watts per m^3 of room volume, which for a normal sized living room will mean an appliance with about a 1.5 kW rating.

(b) *Grade 1 heating:* The following temperatures are required to be maintained in the following rooms:
Living (21°C), Dining (21°C), Kitchen (18°C), Bedroom (16°C), Hall (16°C), Bathroom (21°C), WC (16°C).

(c) *Grade 2 heating:* The following temperatures are required to be maintained in the following rooms:
Living (17°C), Dining (17°C), Kitchen (10°C), Bedroom (10°C), Hall (10°C), Bathroom (10°C), WC (10°C).

(d) *Grade 3 heating:* The following temperatures are required to be maintained in the following rooms:
Living (13°C), Dining (13°C), Kitchen (10°C), Bedroom (10°C), Hall (10°C), Bathroom (10°C), WC (10°C).

BRITISH STANDARD
At the time of writing there is no British Standard for solar assisted heating for domestic hot water, swimming pools or space heating. There is, however, a draft Standard that has been prepared by a technical committee established by the British Standards Institution, and it is due to be published early in 1980. It covers domestic hot water installations only. It will be aimed at the designer and the manufacturer, rather than at the consumer.

BUILT EXAMPLES
- Historical Overview
- Early Heat Pumps
- Catalogue

Historical Overview

INTRODUCTION

The use of solar energy technology is not new. On both sides of the Atlantic, solar activity was flourishing at a time when the United States were torn by civil war and Britain was engaged in Crimea. By the beginning of the twentieth century, domestic solar water heaters as we know them today were in widespread use on the West Coast of America (thirty per cent of Pasadena homes had solar water heaters by 1897) and by the end of World War II, space heating schemes had been developed that used both solar heated air and water.

What *is* new is the public's awareness that solar energy represents a *viable* alternative. The credibility gap has been eliminated in the US, but it will sadly be some time before it can be closed in Europe. This fact is nowhere more clearly emphasised than in the number of solar homes built; well over twenty thousand in the US compared to under thirty in Britain and sadly similar small numbers in the rest of Europe.

The discussion that follows examines the development of solar technology set against the background of alternative energy sources used in Britain.

MEDIEVAL BRITAIN

Wood was the predominant heating fuel. It was in abundant supply in Britain and it was consumed unthinkingly. It was burnt on a stone hearth located in the centre of the room, with a "louvre" or smoke hole in the roof above. Chimneys were gradually introduced, in stone where that was available, and in brick where it was not.

THE AGE OF DISCOVERY 1485—1600

The use of wood as a fuel source declined as it became scarce and expensive, and it was gradually replaced with coal.

For the world it was an age of maritime discovery, personified perhaps by Christopher Columbus who discovered America in 1492. For Elizabethan England, Drake, Hawkins, Frobisher and Raliegh were carving out an Empire. Confidence and enthusiasm were rife. "The patriotic outburst occasioned by the challenge of Spain and the defeat of her Armada (1588) found material expression in the splendid mansion building of the period", as at Hardwick Hall (1576—97) described by contemporaries as "more glass than wall". The forests of England, already ravaged by the wants of the Navy, were now decimated by iron foundries and glass factories as they burnt whole forests for fuel.

England's first energy crisis had arrived. Timber became scarce and expensive, and in some districts, completely used up. Domestic users were forced to turn to "Sea Coale", so called because it was shipped from Newcastle. (The monks of Tynemouth Priory had begun the export of coal from here in about 1296). The demand for coal is reflected in the Newcastle coal export figures: from 33,000 tons in 1563 to 529,000 tons in 1658.

THE SCIENTIFIC REVOLUTION 1600—1700

The wide open fireplaces of the previous centuries — made large enough so that people could sit on either side of the fire to escape the draughts of the room and fully enjoy the radiant heat of both the fire and the masonry surrounds — proved most unsatisfactory for coal. The fire dogs that supported wood would not support coal, so a metal grid and later a grate were introduced to raise the coal off the hearth to permit a draught from below. The burning coal was also extremely offensive. It contained sulphur and understandably the practice of sitting in the fireplace was now abandoned. The spaces on either side were bricked up or reshaped to accept the new metal grates.

59   Orangerie at Holland House, Kensington

The new wave of scientific thought introduced in this era by Hobbes and Newton found expression in many fields of applied technology. Thornburgh patented a method to remove sulphur from coal; coal could now be manufactured into coke; steam power developed from an Italian toy into an English obsession; and the water pump (that proved to be the salvation of the mines) was perfected.

Scientific thought was also applied to the study of nature. This development was led by Renaissance Italy where botanic gardens were established at Pisa (1543), Padua, Florence and Bologna. The great seafaring nations of England and Holland soon followed, establishing their first gardens in Leyden (1587) and Oxford (1621).

In order to protect the plants during the cold months, wintering sheds were erected. Initially they were just timber structures, but they soon became masonry structures with glazed openings. It was these buildings that were to become the typical banqueting halls cum orangeries of the eighteenth century, and the conservatories of the nineteenth century.

60   The Banqueting Hall and Orangery, Kensington Palace, London

THE INDUSTRIAL REVOLUTION 1700–1830

England throbbed with activity: Darby smelted iron using coke (1709); Watt fathered the steam engine (1761); Kay developed the flying shuttle (1733) which led to Hargreaves' spinning jenny (1764); and Cartwright invented the power loom (1785). People moved to the rapidly expanding towns in the North and Midlands to man another British invention, the factory, exemplified perhaps in Arkwright's first cotton factory of 1771. This burst of activity was fuelled by an endless supply of coal.

The expansion of industry meant the availability of cheap coal for everybody. The population that was shifting from rural to urban areas was accommodated in terrace housing, the cheapest form of mass housing known at the time. It was also one that was quite thermally efficient. Being in a terrace, building fabric heat losses were mainly restricted to the front and rear walls, and radiant heat losses from the backs of fireplaces and chimneys were not forfeited to outside, but used to benefit the next-door neighbour. Coal fires were now burning more efficiently in the scientifically designed fireplaces proposed by Count Romford.

The scientific interest in botany, developed in the seventeenth century, was taken up by the aristocratic *amateur* of the eighteenth century. The great botanic hunt was on. The fierce competition to raise exotic species, to bring them to flower or fruit at the earliest possible date, and to have the largest and most varied collection (classifiable by 1753 using Carl Linnaeus' *Species Plantarum*) resulted in the active recruitment of experienced head gardeners and the building of elegant orangeries. By the beginning of the eighteenth century the importance of orientation for these buildings had been fully appreciated. Unlike the Orangery at Holland House (early seventeenth century) where the main axis is north/south, the Orangery at Kensington Palace, built by Christopher Wren in 1704, has its main axis orientated east/west. Glazing is confined to the south facade and it is as extensive as design sensibility would allow. One can only assume that *the greenhouse effect* was fully appreciated. This *greenhouse effect* is achieved when south facing windows permit sunlight to penetrate into the building and warm the structure, yet prevent the heat given off by the floor and internal masonry walls from escaping to the outside. This greenhouse effect is maximised when the building is orientated due south, and the glazing confined to the south side only.

THE EMPIRE 1830–1918

These orangeries of the eighteenth century blossomed into the conservatories of the nineteenth century. Several technological advances made such a development possible: slender wrought iron bars were developed by Loudon (1816); large panes of glass were available from an improved method of broad manufacture developed by R.L. Chance

Historical Overview

in Birmingham on the prompting of Paxton (1832); and the heating of conservatories by piped hot water became practicable. These factors, combined with the lifting of the ninety-nine-year-old glass tax in 1845, resulted in an age of glass structures, such as the Great Conservatory at Chatsworth by Paxton (1836), the Palm House at Kew by Richard Turner and Decimus Burton (1845—48), and of course the Crystal Palace in Hyde Park by Paxton (1851) rebuilt on Sydenham Hill in 1854. During this period a vast body of knowledge and experience was accumulated and used by these designers to create their *artifical climates* with considerable skill, finesse and economy.

But this was not a period when energy economy was an important consideration. Coal continued to be cheap and freely available. The buildings requiring heating were thermally massive (but uninsulated), generally low rise and often in terraces. Once the building had been designed, the heating engineer was then invited to propose a heating scheme. The options available to him were (preferably) a low pressure, gravity fed hot water system, or if that could not be afforded, open coal burning fires. Calculations were based on the worst possible instantaneous heating load (called a steady state calculation) and a high degree of finesse was not required, since the system could be overdesigned in the knowledge that the fuel source — coal — was cheap and abundantly available. It was during this period that the Royal Institute of British Architects (1834), the Royal Institution of Chartered Surveyors (1868) and the Institution of Heating and Ventilating Engineers (1897) were formed.

The nineteenth century also saw a period of intense activity in solar engineering. The new availability of large sheets of glass at reasonable prices, coupled with the scientific enthusiasm and machine mania of the age, produced several solar inventions and applications. Antoine Ponçon applied for the first solar patent in 1854 in London. In 1869, another Frenchman, August Mouchot, published the first book on solar energy "La Chaleur Solaire et Ses Applications Industrielles". Three years later, at a nitrate mine in Las Salines located in the Andes Mountains in Chile, 4756 m^2 of glass were used to distil 19000 litres of water per day, since the local supply was too briny for use. In India, W. Adams, an Englishman, powered a 1.9 kW steam engine with concentrating mirrors in 1876, whilst five years later an American, Professor E.L. Morse of the Lowell Institute in Massachusetts, was granted a patent for a solar air heater that was the precursor of the modern "Trombe" wall. In 1882, the French inventor Pifre drove a printing press with a sun powered steam engine in the Tuileries Gardens, Paris. In America, Clarence M. Kemp patented the "Climax" solar water heater in 1891, that led to the solar boom on the US West Coast from 1895 to 1930, whilst in 1903, another American, Charles Pope, published the first book on solar energy in English called "Solar Heat — Its Practical Applications". By 1909 the "tube and fin" solar collector (identical with today's solar water heater) had been perfected. And in 1913, an English physicist, Professor C.V.R. Boys, joined with an American firm in Egypt to produce a sun powered steam engine (capable of developing 75 kW) that pumped irrigation water from the Nile at Meadi, near Cairo.

The age of the British Empire had also seen the development of the non-renewable fuels. The time honoured and singular fuel source — coal — was introduced to its rivals-to-be, gas and electricity. Gas lighting, first appearing in Pall Mall in 1809, was generally in widespread use by the 1830s. A charter had been granted by 1812 to the "London and Westminster Gas Light and Coke Co." to supply gas light to London. Electricity was also making great leaps forward: the first battery by Volta (1800); the electric motor (1821), then dynamo (1831) by Faraday; the telephone by Bell (1876); the electric light bulb by Swan (1878) and Edison (1879); the first public electric supply in England (1881); the radio by Marconi (1895); the vacuum cleaner by Booth (1901) and the electric washing machine by Fisher (1910).

BETWEEN THE WARS 1918—1939

Despite coal being the overwhelmingly predominant fuel source, electricity use increased rapidly. The six-hundred-plus separate undertakings spread all over Britain were linked together in a *national grid*, set up and operated by the Central Electricity

61   Paxton's "Conservative Wall" at Chatsworth, Derbyshire

Board (itself formed in 1926). The popularity of the electric fire grew (an attitude reinforced by the increasing difficulty in obtaining servants who would lug coal and light fires) and upright gas heaters with fireclay radiants were seen in more and more homes.

Solar activity, however, was limited to the development of the heat pump. The age of the conservatory ended in the 1920's as rising maintenance bills put a halt to the building of new glass structures, and led to the destruction of many existing ones, such as the great Conservatory at Chatsworth in 1920. The end of this era marked the beginning of another. Experimental applications of the heat pump principle were undertaken. Even though Professor Thomson (later Lord Kelvin) had made the theoretical proposal in 1852, no practical realisation had been achieved in a system specifically designed for heating (cooling applications had been achieved by 1881). In the late 1920's, an English engineer, T.G.N. Haldane, made the world's first successful application at his farm in Scotland, where a 5 kW electric motor drove a heat pump that provided hot water for the central heating system as well as the domestic hot water supply. It was not until 1938 that the second British realisation was achieved by S.B. Jackson when he provided heat for his London flat with a heat pump driven by a 3 kW electric motor.

62   The Palm House, Kew Gardens, London

CRISIS TO CRISIS 1939—1973

Britain emerged from World War II with £3000 million in external debts, as well as a depletion of overseas investments to the order of another £1000 million. It was estimated that there was a shortage of 1¼ million homes. Materials were scarce and fuel energy (coal, gas and imported oil) were in short supply. At the "Fuel and the Future" conference held in October 1946, the British pre-war house was described as "the smallest in the civilised world" with all functions of family life confined "to the narrow half circle of warmth in front of the sitting room fire". Since the conference predicted that coal would continue to be the major domestic heating fuel for many years to come, it saw coal-burning efficiency as the *only* area for improvement. To meet the challenge of providing large numbers of houses with fewer resources, new materials and methods of construction were employed: light frames with infill cladding; plasterboard; fibreboard; precast concrete panels; and larger areas of glass. By 1950, the building industry had constructed 800,000 permanent and 148,000 temporary homes.

By the late fifties, however, materials and cheap energy were in plentiful supply. This situation tempted many designers to overlook sensible thermal design considerations as they experimented with new architectural forms. Large areas of glass were orientated in any direction, open planning became the vogue, and lightweight structures (that were usually minimally insulated) permitted new spatial arrangements. The thermal performance of these new buildings was extremely poor, since their lack of insulation and thermal mass made then respond immediately to any outdoor climatic change. They also consumed vast amounts of energy.

The energy they consumed was fossil based and supplied by nationalised bodies: coal (nationalised in 1946); electricity (nationalised in 1947); and gas (nationalised in 1948). During the quarter century following the war the market preference for these three fuel types changed dramatically.

In the early fifties the traditional use of coal in the home was still increasing and it was by far the biggest single fuel source (nearly 320 thousand million kWh equivalent compared to about 15 thousand million for electricity and 40 thousand million for town gas). In fact, so great was the coal consumption in the winters of the early fifties that the fumes created smoky fogs (christened smog in Christmas 1952) so vile and acidic that many Londoners were forced to leave the city. One of these was the English solar pioneer, Edward Curtis, who left Highgate for the cleaner air of Rickmansworth. This intolerable situation in London resulted, understandably, in the Clean Air Acts of the mid fifties and these marked the beginning of the end for coal fires. From 1954 coal use declined gradually until, in 1963, it fell dramatically as the "clean" fuels gained overwhelming popularity.

Historical Overview

From the mid fifties electricity had been promoted as a "clean" fuel. Off peak electric floor warming was advertised as a clean, cost-effective method of space heating. In the quarter century following the War, domestic electricity consumption quadrupled. It was encouraged by an effective pricing policy, supported by an increasing number of generating stations both fossil fuelled and atomic powered, and distributed through a national electricity grid that had been boosted in capacity.

In the same quarter century, gas consumption had also quadrupled. It doubled between the early fifties and 1967, and then, boosted by the supply of North Sea reserves, doubled again between 1967 and 1973.

Oil consumption also increased in this post war period, enjoying particularly favourable periods in the early sixties, the late sixties and the early seventies.

The war years and following decade had also been a time of development for solar energy technology. In the US, the Godfrey L. Cabot bequest to the Massachusetts Institute of Technology (MIT) resulted in the development of four solar assisted space heating schemes between 1939 and 1954. The designers of these schemes (referred to as MIT solar houses I to IV) experimented with roof mounted solar collectors (having areas ranging from $34 \, m^2$ to $60 \, m^2$). Water was used to transfer the collected energy to large water tanks that acted as the heat stores. The team also experimented with designs where the south facade of the building acted as the solar collector, and the building fabric or upright metal water tanks stored the heat. In 1945, in Boulder, Colorado, George Löf designed a system that used air instead of water to transfer the heat from the $43 \, m^2$ of roof mounted solar collector to a $5 \, m^3$ gravel heat store. In 1947, Maria Telkes used containers of glauber salts as an alternative heat store for her air collector system.

In the Mid-West of the US, the Keck brothers were examining the technique of using the building as a solar collector. In the early 1940's, they built several homes in the Chicago area where solar energy came straight into the living space, a heating mode called *direct gain*. This work stimulated Professor F.W. Hutchinson of Purdue University to test two houses during 1945 — one direct gain house and one control house — at Lafayette, Illinois, 130 km south of Chicago. The Libbey—Owens—Ford glass company, based at Toledo, Ohio, 300 kms east of Chicago, also realised the importance of the Keck brothers' work and organised forty-eight highly regarded architects to prepare designs for direct gain solar houses, one for each state then in the US. They were then published in 1947 in a remarkable book entitled "Your Solar House".

During this period of American solar activity, England was also carrying out its own studies.

The development of the British heat pump continued. In 1944, A.C. Pallott developed a 51 kW output unit at Westwood Quarries, where national art treasures were being housed for wartime protection. In 1945, John Sumner commissioned a 235 kW output unit for a corporation building in Norwich, whilst in London, Montagnon and Ruckley had designed the ill-fated 2640 kW output unit for the Royal Festival Hall (1951). In 1952, Miriam Griffith completed the 28 kW output unit for the Shinfield agricultural establishment, and was then involved in several of the large heat pump units installed at electricity generating stations during the mid-fifties. In the late forties, the Radiator Branch of Morris Motors Ltd began experimenting with their standard car radiator to see if it could be used as an efficient heat exchanger when incorporated into an air/air heat pump. The project was abandoned, however, in the mid fifties after about twelve prototypes only had been installed. Finally, during the fifties and sixties John Sumner completed three small heat pump units (12 kW output each) into his own home, located at Norwich.

As well as this heat pump work, developments were also being conducted with roof panel solar collectors. In London, Professor Harold Heywood began experimenting with small areas of solar collectors ($0.1 \, m^2$ in 1947) and then in 1950 began work with complete solar water heating systems. In 1951, he conducted experiments with air, not water, as the heat transfer medium and reported that his results compared favourably with those of the American, Löf, after taking into account the climatic differences.

Work was also being done in England on systems that used the whole building as a solar collector. Prompted by the work of the Keck brothers and others in the US Mid-West, N.S. Billington from the Building Research Station at Garston near London examined the possibilities of such systems in the British climate. In 1947, he concluded that the use of large south facing windows that act as solar collectors was not effective. What he failed to appreciate at the time, in common with his American contemporaries, was the vital role played by highly insulated movable shutters. Used at night these can reduce heat losses by up to 70%, and make the south facing window a net energy gainer, rather than a net energy loser.

Similar work was done at another Building Research Station at Abbots Langley in the early fifties. This study showed that when a reasonably insulated standard house is used as a solar collector, solar energy could contribute 4700 kWh of heat during the winter months, even though 45 per cent of this heat was obtained in just two of these months. At a meeting held in 1954, J.K. Page suggested that this solar gain could be maximised by storing the collected energy in the mass of the interior walls (that were externally insulated) and that night-time heat losses could be reduced by using double glazing in conjunction with curtains.

The built results of this experimental solar work were meagre. They are fully documented in Chapter 10 (use the *italicised names* as references) but in summary they consist of only four houses and a school. All five of these use the building as the solar collector. In 1956, the two storey *Curtis House* was built, and included $28 \, m^2$ of

south facing window to provide heat for the 139 m^2 floor plan. In 1961, the *Wallasey School* was constructed with 877 m^2 of the south facing glazing to heat the classrooms and ancillary teaching spaces, and it is still one of the world's largest solar buildings. In 1968, the three storey **Summers House** used 49 m^2 of south facing glazing for its 156 m^2 plan area, while the L-shaped single storey **Thame Farmhouse** (1970) has 25 m^2 of effecting south facing glazing for its 113 m^2 floor plan area. The fifth example, however, used an 88 m^2 conservatory attached to the south side of the building to collect its solar energy. It was the **Street Farmhouse** erected in 1973, but demolished two years later in 1975.

These were small pickings from such a fertile tree. Sadly, the crop had been blighted somewhat by misunderstanding and inexperience, but mainly by the presence of cheap and plentiful fossil fuels that were consumed unthinkingly.

This age of thoughtless energy consumption ended in 1973 as the Organisation of Petroleum Exporting Countries (OPEC) took a new stance. In November 1973, the Secretary-General of OPEC remarked at a conference on the North Sea in Houston, Texas:

I am of the opinion that we have to commence to give oil a real value, i.e. consider it as a precious wealth, expensive by definition and subject to protection from any wasteful usage. We believe, indeed, that a high-price policy could serve the function of preventing such wastage and in addition that a reduction in production could serve the same goal . . . such a reduction should be adopted by all producing countries.

(SOURCE: *Petroleum Times*, 16 November 1973)

63 Curtis House, Rickmansworth

64 Summers House, Blackheath, London

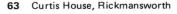

65 Wallasey School, Cheshire

66 Thame Farmhouse, Oxfordshire

Historical Overview

THE SOLAR AWAKENING — POST 1974

This new attitude to energy being a finite resource with a price tag that reflected its precious value saw an immediate and understandable reaction to enact a policy of energy conservation. The Department of Energy was formed in 1975 and instituted a "Save It" campaign in 1976. The Royal Institute of British Architects introduced a long life/loose fit/low energy policy. The thermal requirements of The Building Regulations were improved, first for domestic dwellings (1975) and subsequently for all heated buildings (1979). Innumerable energy related organisations were formed during the aftermath of the energy crisis.

A second reaction was to investigate solar energy, since the higher prices now being demanded for the fossil based fuels were making the economics of solar technology vastly more attractive. These investigations were carried out by both private individuals and large organisations.

(Their work is summarised below, but it is reported in far greater detail in Chapter 10, reference to which can be made by using the *italicised names* below.)

Due to almost non-existence Government assistance, the number of private research projects involving complete buildings was restricted to four. Of these, three were houses that used an attached conservatory to provide solar heat: Robert and Brenda Vale at *The Horse and Gate* (a pub they converted into a house from 1973 to 1978); Cedric Green at a house in Suffolk called *Delta* (1974); and John Shore and Frances Pulling at Brighton with the *Integrated Solar Dwelling* (1977). The fourth project was at the National Centre for Alternative Technology (NCAT) and used 98 m^2 of solar collector and an immense water store in an attempt to provide 100% solar heating for the *NCAT Exhibition Hall* (1976).

Other equally concerned people financed solar heating schemes that were for their own use, but which were not intended as experiments. J.B. Wright installed 33 m^2 of solar collector on the roof of his *Anglesey House* (1975); the design team for the *Macclesfield House* collected solar energy in an attached greenhouse (1976), as did the designers for the *Huddaknowl House* and the *Dudgeon House* (1978); the two homes of Clive *Plumb* and Brian *Wilson* used combinations of heat pumps and solar collectors (1977); and the *Kippford House* became Britain's first space heating system using air collectors (1979).

Some commercial organisations saw a potential market and built prototypes to test their products. The Calor Group Ltd tested 54 m^2 of solar collector linked to a variety of thermal stores at *Fulmer* (1976); Design and Materials Ltd included in their plan range a house that incorporated 40 m^2 of solar collector, a built example being at *Blyth* (1976); and *Wates* Ltd, the national house builder, erected a low energy/heat

pump room at NCAT (1976). Of these three companies who saw a potential market in "solar", only one, the Calor Group Ltd are still proceeding with the their product development.

In an effort to combat the rising costs of fuel, Councils and Development Corporations began experimenting with homes and schools. The inaugurator was the Milton Keynes Development Corporation (MKDC) who installed in the *Milton Keynes House* 37 m^2 of solar collector (1975). They are now continuing their investigations with housing schemes at *Pennyland* and *Linford 8B* where the building itself is used as the solar collector. This solar collection technique is also used at the *Higher Bebington* development by the Merseyside Improved Houses housing association (1978), as well as at the *Northlands 1* site developed by the Basildon Development Corporation (1979). However, the *Livingston* Development Corporation (1978) and the city of *Salford* (1979) used heat pumps in their housing experiments. Heat pumps were also used by the Essex County Council at the *Roach Vale School* (1977) and at *Walton "The Gunfleet" Tendring High School* (under construction). Cheshire County Council, however, chose to use 40 m^2 of solar collector for the *Sandbach County Primary School* (1977) and with the experience gained, are now installing 200 m^2 of collector to help heat the elderly persons' home at *Shavington* (under construction).

Since 1973, twenty-two solar assisted space heating schemes have been completed in Britain. Eighteen have involved houses, three have involved small County Primary Schools, and the remaining one is an exhibition hall at the National Centre for Alternative Technology.

Of the thirteen solar assisted space heating schemes under construction at the time of writing eleven involve houses and two, small County Primary Schools.

67   Higher Bebington housing development, Merseyside

It would appear therefore that in Britain solar assisted space heating schemes have not gained widespread credibility. The buildings involved are still small in scale, and almost exclusively limited to domestic and educational use. They are still mainly being built for evaluation purposes. They are not spread evenly over the country, but are still limited to two main areas (south-east England and the Liverpool/Manchester area).

The situation now is Britain is in some ways similar to one that existed in the US during the mid seventies. There were relatively few built examples, they were mostly small in scale and limited in user type, and they had not gained public credibility. Now at the turn of the decade, there are over twenty thousand American solar buildings that cover a vast spectrum of user type. Public credibility has been achieved. This last point is clearly evidenced by the ever increasing number of coffee table publications that sumptuously document the now common American middle class solar home.

A number of factors have helped contribute to this transformation. Amongst such factors are Government funded demonstration projects, tax incentives, Government financial aid, legislation of solar rights, solar competitions, solar conferences, national information sources, and solar schools. Northern Europe has much to learn from the American experience.

The next five years in Britain could well be critical to the development of solar assisted space heating schemes. Only time will tell if the fruitful start as documented in the following Catalogue has been correctly nurtured, or whether it has been left to rot on the tree at the expense of other seemingly more attractive options that may well prove to have a bitter core.

BIBLIOGRAPHY USED FOR THIS CHAPTER

1   ADAMSON, GARETH. *Machines at Home.* Lutterworth Press, 1969.
2   ARMYTAGE, W.H.G. *A Social History of Engineering.* Faber and Faber, 1961.
3   BANHAM, REYNER. *The Architecture of the Well-tempered Environment.* Architectural Press, 1969.
4   BILLINGTON, N.S. 'Solar Heat Gain through Windows', *Journal of the Royal Institute of British Architects* pp 177–180, January 1947.
5   BRONOWSKI, J. *The Common Sense of Science.* Heinemann, 1951.
6   BRUNSKILL, R.W. *Vernacular Architecture.* Faber and Faber, 1971.
7   *Energy* Central Office of Information Reference Pamphlet 124, HMSO, 1975.
8   *Energy for the future* The Institute of Fuel, 1972.
9   *Energy Resources.* Prepared by the Open University for Science: A Second Level Course, The Open University Press, 1973.
10 FLETCHER, SIR BANISTER. *A History of Architecture.* B.T. Batsford Ltd, 1954
11 FOLEY, GERALD. *The Energy Question.* Pelican, 1976.
12 'Fuel and the Future'. Report on Conference. *Journal of the Royal Institute of British Architects* pp 3–30, November 1946.
13 GIEDION, SIEGFRIED. *Mechanization Takes Command.* Oxford University Press, 1948.
14 HEYWOOD, H. 'Solar Energy for Water and Space Heating'. *Journal of the Institute of Fuel* 27, pp 334–347, July 1954.
15 HIX, JOHN. *The Glass House.* The MIT Press, 1974.
16 KINGSFORD, P.W. *Builders and Building Workers.* Edward Arnold, 1973.
17 LLOYD, NATHANIEL. *History of the English House.* Architectural Press, 1975.
18 McVEIGH, J.C. *Sun Power.* Pergamon Press, 1977.
19 PALMER, R.R. *Historical Atlas of the World.* Rand McNally, 1965.
20 TARN, J.N. *Working-class Housing in 19th-Century Britain.* Lund Humphries, 1971.
21 TAYLOR, DUNCAN. *A Short History of the Post War World 1945–1970.* Dobson Books Ltd, 1977.
22 THOMPSON, HUGH. *Engineers and Engineering.* B.T. Batsford Ltd, 1976.
23 WILLIAMS, BRIAN. *Inventions and Discoveries.* Franklin Watts, 1978.
24 YELLOTT, J.I. 'Solar Energy: Its Use And Control'. *Heating, Piping and Air Conditioning,* September 1966, October 1966, March 1967, April 1967.

68 Port Isaac County Primary Schoo, Cornwall

Early Heat Pumps

INTRODUCTION

As explained in general in the historical overview, there was considerable activity in the development of heat pumps in Britain around the time of World War II. Up till that time there had been little activity in the field since the middle of the previous century. Scarcely one year after Joseph Paxton had delighted the English people with the Crystal Palace and demonstrated that solar assisted passive space heating was possible on an immense scale, Professor William Thomson (later Lord Kelvin) published an article in the December 1852 proceedings of the Glasgow Philosophical Society titled "On the Economy of Heating and Cooling of Buildings by Means of Currents of Air" which, along with an accompanying paper, outlined the operation of a machine known as a heat pump. Though by 1881 the principle had been applied successfully to cooling, it was not until another fifty years had passed that it was successfully applied to heating.

HALDANE FARM

The first successful application of the heat pump was designed and installed in the late 1920's by T.G.N. Haldane, a partner in the consulting engineering firm of Merz and McLellan. The system was located at Haldane's farm in Scotland and provided hot water for both the central space heating panel radiators as well as the domestic hot water system. The 5 kW electric motor that drove the system was powered by a small hydro-electric installation, which also provided power and light to both Haldane's and two other neighbouring farms. The source of heat for the heat pump was outside air, which was augmented in cold weather by heat taken in from cold water flowing through a tank of water containing another evaporator for the heat pump. Haldane's paper on this work attracted world wide attention, particularly in America and Switzerland, which lead to several commercial installations being made in those two countries.

JACKSON HOUSE

The second British installation of a heat pump was a small system installed in the London flat of S.B. Jackson during 1938. A 3 kW motor drove a four cylinder compressor to provide heat for the 240 m^3 space, that had a peak heat loss rate of about 10 kW. Sadly, after over three years of successful operation, it "disappeared in the events of 1941".

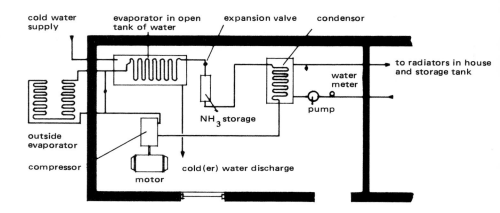

69 Plan of equipment at the Haldane farm

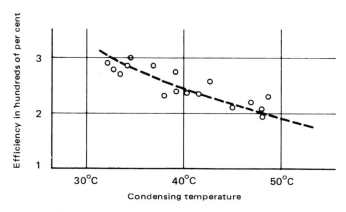

70 Test results of Haldene's experimental heat pump (Evaporating temperature at -6.7°C)

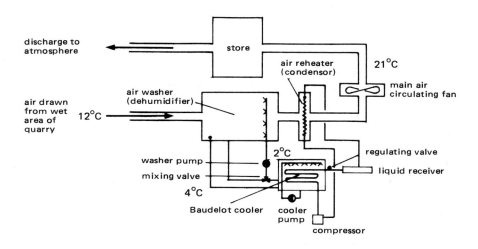

discharge to atmosphere

store

air reheater (condensor)

21°C

main air circulating fan

air washer (dehumidifier)

air drawn from wet area of quarry

12°C

washer pump

mixing valve

2°C

4°C

regulating valve

liquid receiver

Baudelot cooler

cooler pump

compressor

71 Modified plant layout at Westwood Quarries

72 General view of Norwich heat pump showing compressor and evaporator

WESTWOOD QUARRIES

It was also during the Second World War that the third installation occurred. Enemy bombing threatened the contents of England's national museums and art galleries, and two subterranean sites were selected and adapted to provide for the safekeeping of these treasures. One of the sites provided 2300 m^2 of storage space in underground caverns, that had naturally occurring temperatures of 11°C and which were completely saturated. The original airhandling scheme dehumidified the saturated cavern air with electrically powered airconditioning units, then heated it with coal fired boilers. Running costs were £3380 per annum. In 1944, A.C. Pallot rearranged the existing airconditioning plant (that operated on a heat pump principle) so that waste heat from the dehumidifying section was used to heat the air, instead of using coal fired boilers. Running costs were halved and the coal fired boilers shut down. The 51.3 kW output plant was dismantled after the war when the art treasures were returned to their original locations.

NORWICH HEAT PUMP

In 1940 the five storey, 4000 m^2 workshop and office building for the Norwich Corporation Electricity Department in Duke St., Norwich, was nearing completion and the heating plant to satisfy the 235 kW demand was still to be decided. Tenders for a heat pump designed to the specification of J.A. Sumner were forwarded to each British manufacturer of refrigeration plant, but sadly no completed tenders were received (most probably due to the wartime restrictions). Consequently coal fired boilers were installed and operated until 1945. But by October of that year, Sumner had succeeded in building and completing the specified heat pump by his own endeavours, using mainly second-hand and salvaged materials. From this time, the 60 kW heat pump was used exclusively to heat the building, using the adjacent River Wensum as the source of heat. Seasonal reciprocal efficiencies of about 3.5 were obtained. On nationalisation in 1947, the Corporation was taken over by the Eastern Electricity Board, who viewed the heat pump with suspicion and sadly dismantled it in 1951 after six years of trouble free service.

Early Heat Pumps

SHIPS

During the war the German Navy had fitted several small heat pumps to their Type 21 submarines, and a number of these were sent to Britain for evaluation. After three trial installations in British submarines, the Admiralty decided in 1947 to install a 61 kW heat pump in the HMS Vidal, a diesel driven survey ship. During the 1950's the largest sea-going installation was probably the 710 kW heat pump system used on the ocean liner the Southern Cross.

ELECTRICAL RESEARCH ASSOCIATION (ERA)

In 1947 the ERA, acting on the suggestion of one of its councillors, T.G.N. Haldane (see above), set up a small research team at the ERA laboratory at Leatherhead, Surrey to investigate the performance of small (3.7 kW) heat pumps, as well as the suitability of various sources of low grade heat (air, water and soil). The results of this important work are recorded in reports held at the ERA library, which is still located at Leatherhead.

MORRIS MOTORS LTD (RADIATOR BRANCH)

In 1948 the Morris Motors Ltd (Radiator Branch) decided to become involved in heat pumps with the aim of utilizing their car radiators as efficient heat exchangers. About twelve prototype heat pumps were made, each with a 3 kW drive motor, and installed in various buildings for staff, friends and relatives, mainly around Cowley. One system was installed for John Laing (R & D) in a Laing home built north of London. Outside air was generally used as the heat source (though it appears that ground coils were used in two installations) and heat was distributed within the houses via polythene tubing (an innovation at the time) embedded in the floor slabs. A C.O.P. of about three was obtained, and defrosting was automatic in winter. The units were quite large, being about 1.5 metres high and 1.8 by 0.9 metres in plan. The ERA (see above) became involved in the project in the mid fifties, but the scheme was abandoned in about 1956 because it was felt that the market was not great enough to warrant the sales and development effort required.

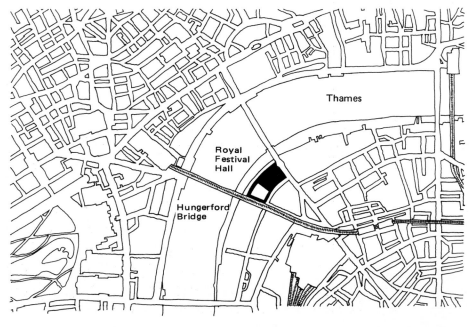

73 Map showing location of Royal Restival Hall, London

Early Heat Pumps

74 Plan of Sumner house

75 Royal Festival Hall, London, with Hungerford Bridge on right

SUMNER HOUSE

Having completed the Norwich heat pump in 1945, it was only natural that Sumner's newly built house that he occupied in 1950 should employ a heat pump in the heating system. He designed and built two heat pump systems between 1950 and 1960, and a third one, still operating most satisfactorily, in 1961. The two bedroom, 153 m² single storey brick house was designed well to the front of the plot in order to leave the land to the south free for a generous sunny garden as well as space to bury the heat pump ground coil. This ground coil consists of 200 metres of small diameter piping that draws heat from the earth, the earth acting as a heat store that is constantly being replenished by the sun. A 4 kW electric motor drives the heat pump that distributes heat via an underfloor heating system, consisting of 10 mm copper pipes cast 50 mm into the 125 mm screed at 300 mm centres. Each room is separately supplied from a main header system that is fitted with a set of isolating valves. The system is still operating perfectly with an annual coefficient of performance of about three.

ROYAL FESTIVAL HALL

Towards the end of 1948, in a decision no doubt stimulated by the work of Sumner and the ERA, the newly appointed Chief Scientist's Division of the Ministry of Fuel and Power assumed an interest in heat pumps, and the mooted Royal Festival Hall, soon to be built at the Festival of Britain site on the South Bank of the Thames, was selected for an experimental installation. The designers, P. Montagnon and A. Ruckley, arranged that the system was to be run in parallel with the traditional gas fired boiler system in order to obtain comparative results. Two gas fired, converted and derated Merlin aircraft engines provided 521 kW of power to drive the heat pumps, that used river water drawn from the centre of the Thames as the source of heat. The heat pump plant was installed in the brick arch of the Hungerford railway bridge nearest to the river so as not to interfere with the design of the Festival Hall. The London County Council architect's department had advised the designers that the peak heat loss rate would be 7325 kW, so the heat pump was sized to provide 2640 kW in order to ensure a continual base load running condition for the heat pump system. However, due to the high level of thermal insulation that was provided by the acoustic insulation, and the large heat emission of the occupants, the maximum peak heat loss rate did not exceed 2000 kW. Because of the plant design, the system could only be used for pre-heating for short periods of time. Ready for use in June 1951, the equipment was dismantled in 1954 and the plant room converted to a store. The gas fired boilers were then used exclusively to heat the building. The bad publicity generated by this installation stifled once again the commercial acceptance of the heat pump.

Early Heat Pumps

SHINFIELD

In order to gain some practical experience to back their theoretical knowledge, the ERA research committee designed and installed in 1952 a 7.5 kW input heat pump at the ERA agricultural establishment at Shinfield, five kilometres from Reading. The system was designed by Miriam Griffith who headed the ERA heat pump team. Previous work at Leatherhead (see above) had established that heat could be extracted from the ground at a rate of 33 watts per linear metre, using 20 mm copper piping spaced at least 300 mm apart, and buried at a depth between one and two metres. Since the surface area available at the Establishment was not sufficient to provide all the heat required, a twenty cubic metre buried tank (ten metres long) was also installed. This heating system operated satisfactorily for ten years until the establishment was taken over by the Reading University.

POWER STATIONS

During the early fifties, as Britain increased the capacity of its national electrical grid, many new power stations were built and an interest was shown by their designers in utilizing heat pumps to recover heat from the generating station's cooling outfall water. (Amongst those designers was the ubiquitous name of Haldane.) Most of the installations provided heating for the workshops and offices. The author is aware of four such installations, though probably more exist: *Stourport* in Worcestershire (two systems of 95 kW and 220 kW outputs that have both now been dismantled); *Meaford* in Staffordshire (a 132 kW output system that operated satisfactorily until the whole station was shut down in 1975); *Cowes* on the Isle of Wight (a 67 kW output system installed in 1954 and operated satisfactorily for about ten years until the declining use of the station made the heat pump operation inappropriate. The plant was dismantled when the station was demolished in 1976); and *Great Yarmouth* (a 490 kW output system installed in 1957 and dismantled after about three years because of maintenance problems).

THE LUCAS AEROSPACE COMPANY

At the end of the fifties and the beginning of the sixties the Lucas Company attempted to create a market for domestic heat pumps. It developed an efficient air/air heat pump and installed them in two houses just outside Burnley. The systems were designed by J. A. Sumner. After two years of monitoring, the results were forwarded to the Electricity Boards who showed remarkably little interest. Approximately one hundred machines (2.2 kW and 3.7 kW) were sold, but the product was dropped in 1964 as Lucas concentrated on other areas of activity.

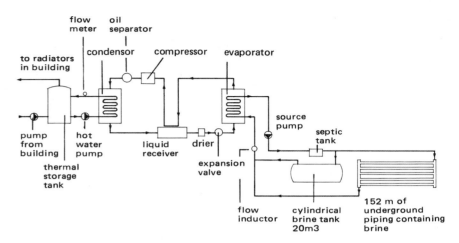

76 Schematic layout of heat pump installation at Shinfield, Berkshire

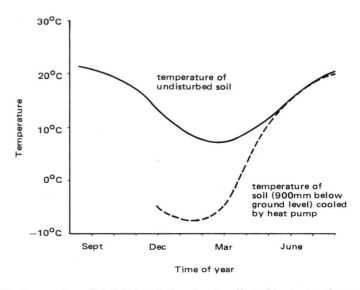

77 Test results at Shinfield installation showing effect of heat extracting on ground temperatures

NUFFIELD COLLEGE

Nuffield College in Oxford was founded in 1937 and by 1954 the heating system came up for review. With a public awareness of the potential of heat pumps, the College held discussions with Mr. G. Dono of Morris Motors Ltd (Radiator Branch), Mr. J.A. Sumner and Mr. P.E. Montagnon. The outcome of these discussions was a proposal for an air/water heat pump. However, after the involvement of Oscar Faber and Partners, it was finally agreed to use city sewerage as the heat source instead of air; tests discovered that the temperature of the sewerage only varied between 43°C and 58°C, and it was available at a fairly constant flow. A diesel driven engine powered the heat pump that was housed in a small plant room (9.5 m by 6.9 m), that was distant from the College. The sewerage was taken from the existing barrel drain, pumped to an annular heat exchanger, where the extracted heat was transferred to water that was pumped to the main boiler in the College buildings. The slightly cooled sewerage (a drop of only 5°C was permitted) was then returned to the sewer drain. The output of the heat pump is 127 kW and effects an oil fuel saving of 112 kW equivalent. The system was commissioned in 1961/62, but is not operating at the present time.

BIBLIOGRAPHY USED FOR THIS CHAPTER

1   GRIFFITH, M.V. 'Some Aspects of Heat Pump Operation in Great Britain'. *IEE Proceedings* Vol 104, Part A, June 1957.
2   GRIFFITH, M.V. 'Heat Pump Progress in Great Britain'. *Direct Current*, March 1960.
3   GRIFFITH, M.V. 'Application of the Heat Pump in Great Britain'. *Research Applied to Industry*, February 1961.
4   GRIFFITH, M.V. 'Heat Pump Potential'. *Built Environment*, July 1974.
5   HALDANE, T.G.N. 'The Heat Pump — An Economical Method of Producing Low-grade Heat from Electricity'. *Journal of the IEE*, p 666, Vol 68, 1930.
6   KELL, J.R. and MARTIN, P.L. 'The Nuffield College Heat Pump'. *Journal of the Institution of Heating and Ventilating Engineers*, January 1963.
7   MONTAGNON, P.E. and RUCKLEY, A.L. 'The Festival Hall Heat Pump'. *Journal of the Institute of Fuel*, April 1954.
8   PALLOT, A.C. 'A Heat Pump Installation'. *Journal of the Institution of Heating and Ventilating Engineers*, May—June 1946.
9   SUMNER, J.A. 'The Norwich Heat Pump', *Journal of the Institution of Mechanical Engineers*, Vol 158, No. 1, June 1948.
10   SUMNER, J.A. *Domestic Heat Pumps*. Prism Press, 1976.

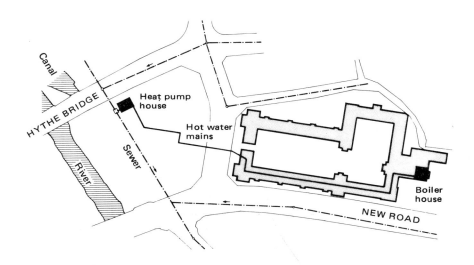

78   Site plan of Nuffield College, Oxford

Catalogue

The buildings catalogued in this chapter have been selected with two main criteria in mind: firstly, that the examples have been built and occupied before the middle of 1979; and secondly, that they are "solar buildings". Solar buildings under construction at the time of writing have been included in summary form at the end of the chapter.

The term "solar building" is difficult to define. Essentially it denotes those buildings that make use of the sun's energy to satisfy a significant proportion of their space heating loads, thus reducing the amount of fossil fuel required to make good the remainder. Heat pumps have been included in this category since they reduce the amount of fossil fuel required to heat a space by extracting solar energy stored in the earth, the air and bodies of water (lakes, rivers, streams etc). All of the early examples of heat pumps have been noted in the previous chapter, but for recent years, only a selection of the significant examples have been listed, since the use of the heat pump is now relatively widespread (perhaps in the order of five hundred installations).

The examples catalogued has been grouped according to heating mode in Table (79) opposite. It is interesting to note the emphasis on heat pumps, direct gain and liquid flat plate collectors.

The material used to prepare the catalogue is a pot-pourri of journal and magazine articles, information gleaned from other relevant written sources, interviews with the architects, the solar engineers and the occupants, and site visits. Most of the technical information has been provided directly by the consultants, and when considering this information, the reader must bear this source in mind.

It is hoped that the author has not omitted any deserving example. If so, it is not through contempt, but rather that he was unaware of its existence. The author would be most pleased to receive information about any such examples, so that they can be included in future editions of the book.

	1950	1960	1970	1980	1990
Direct gain	1 ●	2 ●	3 4 ● ●	25 ●	
Thermal storage wall				21 ●	
Solar greenhouse			5 6 10 18 ●● ● ●●)		
Roof pond				22 23 26	
Convective loop				11 12 16 19	
Liquid flat plate collector			7 8 9 ●) ●●))		
Air flat plate collector				27 ●	
Concentrating collector					
Heat pump				13 17 24 ●●●	
Solar assisted heat pump				14 15 20 ●●●	

79 Table cataloguing examples by heating mode. (for reference to example numbers, see listing on opposite page)

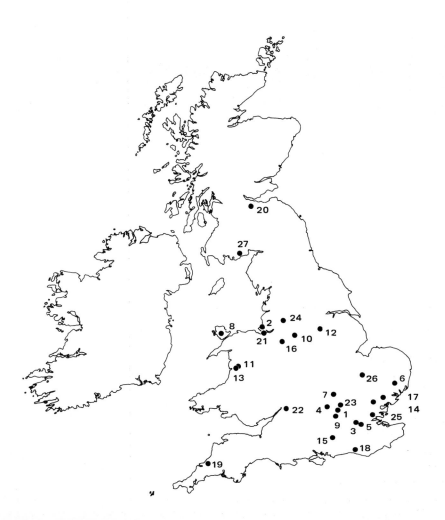

1 CURTIS HOUSE
2 WALLASEY SCHOOL
3 SUMMERS HOUSE
4 THAME FARMHOUSE
5 STREET FARMHOUSE
6 DELTA
7 MILTON KEYNES HOUSE
8 ANGLESEY HOUSE
9 FULMER LABORATORY
10 MACCLESFIELD HOUSE
11 NCAT EXHIBITION HALL
12 BLYTH HOUSE
13 WATES HOUSE
14 PLUMB HOUSE
15 WILSON HOUSE
16 SANDBACH COUNTY PRIMARY SCHOOL
17 ROACH VALE COUNTY PRIMARY SCHOOL
18 INTEGRATED SOLAR DWELLING
19 PORT ISAAC COUNTY PRIMARY SCHOOL
20 LIVINGSTON HOUSE
21 HIGHER BEBINGTON HOUSES
22 HUDDAKNOWL HOUSE
23 DUDGEON HOUSE
24 SALFORD HOUSES
25 NORTHLANDS 1 HOUSING
26 THE HORSE AND GATE HOUSE
27 KIPPFORD HOUSE

80 Map showing location of catalogues examples

CURTIS HOUSE

Address:	9 Beacon Way, Rickmansworth, Hertfordshire
Architect:	Edward J.W. Curtis
Solar engineer:	Edward J.W. Curtis and Allan S. Miller
Date occupied:	November 1956

Edward Curtis had many interests. He was an educator, lecturing at Leicester School of Architecture from 1949 to 1951, and then at the Polytechnic of North London from 1951 onwards. He was also concerned with art and the integration of art and technology. His Rickmansworth house contained many of his own paintings, a mural in the entrance hall, a delicate purpose-made welded steel staircase, an outdoor sculpture, and a colour scheme that emphasised the large abstract patterns created by the building's structure itself. Curtis also saw potential in prefabrication and component design. He worked as a consultant with Plyglass Ltd, from 1954 to 1963, in the development of insulating glass, window frames and multi-material wall panels. All of these were used at Rickmansworth. The flexibility of internal spaces also intrigued Curtis. The outer shell of his two storey Rickmansworth home is economically defined by two brick side walls on the east and the west, with the north and south openings being filled with prefabricated glazed screens. Within this small space, only 11.2 by 6.1 metres in plan, there is a surprisingly spacious and airy feeling. The ground floor is mostly open planned with a double-height void on the south, while the first floor is subdivided into bedrooms by non-structural, full height, movable storage units. Curtis was also an innovator. Unlike other designers in the early 1950's he was concerned with the economic use of then reasonably priced electricity and the integration of solar energy. Apart from his own house at Rickmansworth (1956), he designed the Mettam house at Blyth, Nottinghamshire that incorporated a 2.25 m^2 solar collector for preheating domestic hot water (1964), a 36 m^2 trickle type solar collector for a private swimming pool at Westerham, Kent (1967), and the Solar Dome House for the Ideal Home Exhibition at Olympia (1970).

The site of the Curtis house was selected for two reasons. Firstly, for health reasons, since Curtis had been forced to leave his London home because of the smogs of the early 1950's and Rickmansworth provided clean air. Secondly, the site was located high on the north side of the Colne River valley, and thus provided an unobstructed sun path as well as a spectacular view of the river valley below. The house was initially refused planning permission because "it was too modern for the area", but this decision was later overturned by Ministerial inquiry.

ENERGY CONSERVATION
The 132 m^2 building is wrapped in an aluminium foil blanket that rises vertically up the centre of the brick cavity wall (U-value of 1.1 W/m^2°C) and across the top of the ceiling joists (U-value of 0.62 W/m^2°C). The three main window wall units and two small bedroom windows are double glazed (U-value of 3.2 to 3.7 W/m^2°C) while other non-glazed insulated infill panels are Vitroslab (U-value of 2.3 to 2.5 W/m^2°C) and resin bonded plywood panels (U-value of 0.79 W/m^2°C). Movable insulation to the south window wall is provided by two layers of curtains (light and heavy). The building is temperature zoned, provided with a draught lobby, and has controlled ventilation. The peak heat loss rate is 8.3 kW and the specific heat loss rate 415 W/°C.

PASSIVE HEATING
Direct gain heating is employed. The collector area is 28 m^2 of glazing facing 22° east of south and sized at 20% of the floor area. Internal brickwork and the concrete floor act as thermal storage. Curtains provide movable insulation. No overhang was provided for summer protection, but the curtaining provides some relief.

ACTIVE HEATING
A heat pump system is employed. The 12 kW output unit was located in a small room lined with acoustic tiles. The machine initially was a water/air unit, but after one year's operation it was converted, because of defrosting problems, to an air/air unit. Supply air was circulated in uninsulated ceiling ducts with return air being drawn through an underfloor duct via open spaces and 38 mm gaps below all doors. The control panel was in the kitchen. The system could also be used for summer cooling. Recently the heat pump machinery needed to be replaced, but for a variety of reasons, the scheme was abandoned and instead a conventional heating system was installed.

PERFORMANCE
No measured data is available, but Curtis estimates that the average annual electrical consumption was 8590 kWh (day tariff) and 1510 kWh (night tariff), a total of 10,100 kWh. This represents 76 kWh per m^2 of floor area for a system that provided year round temperature control. Performance could be improved by the use of better movable insulation and the erection of shading devices to prevent summer overheating.

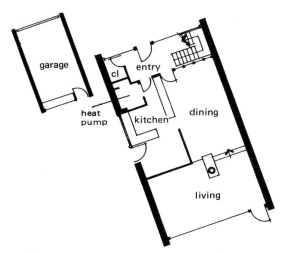

81 Ground floor plan

garage

cl entry

heat pump

kitchen

dining

living

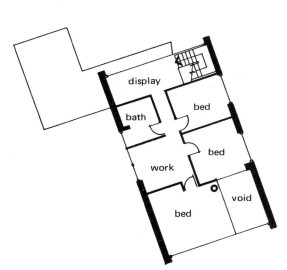

82 First floor plan

display

bath

bed

work

bed

bed

void

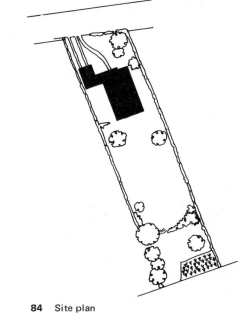

84 Site plan

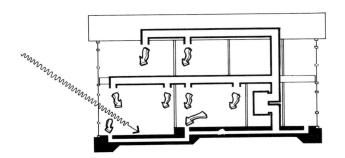

83 Section

85 South elevation showing large collector area of double-height windows

Catalogue

WALLASEY SCHOOL ✳

Address:	St George's County Secondary School, Leasowe Road, Wallasey, Cheshire.
Architect:	Emslie A Morgan
Solar engineer:	Emslie A Morgan
Date occupied:	September 1961

Emslie Morgan was a quiet, cagey Scotsman. Educated in Aberdeen, he joined the architect's department at Wallasey in about 1946/47. At that time he was aware of the solar work being done as the Massachusetts Institute of Technology and had received literature from them. He was the complete architect being able not only to design, document and administer a building, but also capable of completing the design and calculations for the structure, the electrical layout, and the heating and ventilating system. He was considered by his co-workers to be eccentric but brilliant, poor in committee, but excellent in science. As senior assistant for school projects to the Borough Architect, W. P. Clayton, Morgan was the project architect for the first stage of the St George's County Secondary School. It was completed in 1955. In 1959 he was asked to complete the second stage of the building, expanding the school from 300 to 600 students. However, after Morgan had completed the documentation of the conventionally designed Annexe, trial bores holes revealed that expensive footings would be required for this part of the site. Morgan was therefore asked to quickly redesign for another part of the site. Working alone, Morgan now produced his radical solar design. Both the Borough Architect and his deputy, C.A. Caven, were somewhat shocked. Time did not permit yet another redesign, and reluctantly, the solar scheme was approved. On completion, however, world wide publicity was attracted to the building, the architect and the Council. It was only after this publicity that the Architect's Department sought Council approval for the £17,000 that the contract was over yardstick. It was granted without hesitation.

In April 1961, Morgan applied for a patent for his solar heating ideas and was thus prevented from publishing any data about them. Instead he tried to obtain a Government grant (similar to the one given to the Hovercraft) to develop and sell his own ideas. He was unsuccessful. On his death in 1964, Morgan's executor attempted to set up a consortium, but this venture also came to nothing.

The school is sited on the north side of more than one kilometre of drained land that is now used as the sport's field. This provides the building with an unobstructed sun path. The two storey building has a plan area of 2200 m^2, 1330 m^2 of which is used as teaching space.

ENERGY CONSERVATION

The building shell is heavily insulated. The 180 mm concrete roof and 230 mm external brick walls are covered with 130 mm of polystyrene (U-values of 0.22 and 0.23 $W/m^2{}^oC$ respectively), then waterproof roofing felt. The 150 mm ground floor slab is covered with a 100 mm screed. The solar wall has an overall U-value of 3.1 $W/m^2{}^oC$. The plan is temperature zoned and the connecting corridor on the north side acts as a draught lobby. Ventilation rates are kept low in winter. Occupants find this environment satisfactory, but some visitors have noted a certain staleness.

PASSIVE HEATING

Both direct gain and thermal storage wall heating modes are used. The direct gain solar wall provided for the west wing of the Annexe is 71.5 m long by 8.2 m high and orientated 20° west of south. This wall is made up of an outer layer of clear glass and an inner layer, 610 mm away, of both diffuse glass (88%) and black painted masonry (12%). Small areas of the solar wall have reversible panels that can be faced shiny side out April to October and black side out November to March. The clumsiness and ineffectiveness of this system results in the panels rarely being reversed. The solar wall to east wing of the Annexe is 32 m long and 5.2 m to 8.2 m in height. It is orientated 10° east of south. Two lengths of non-vented Trombe wall are located in the gymnasium, and are separated from the translucent solar wall sections by vertical perspex panels. Ventilator filter boxes at the base of all the solar walls eliminate condensation, and three levels of walkway tracks provide access for maintenance etc, as well as baffling large convection currents that might be set up. The woodwork room has 27.6 m^2 of solar wall at clerestorey level. Overall there is 877 m^2 of south facing solar wall. For the classrooms, the collector to floor area ratio is typically 0.42. Thermal storage for all spaces is provided mostly in the massive floors and ceilings.

PERFORMANCE

An oil-fired space heating system was installed at the insistence of the financing authority, but it has rarely been used. The solar wall appears to contribute 25% to 30% of the space heating load [2] [7] with the balance being provided by the occupants and the tungsten lighting (24 W/m^2 of floor area). The combined heating and lighting costs of the solar building have been estimated to be 63% of those of the conventional building [3], and the capital costs reckoned to be much the same [4]. A far more comprehensive report is soon to be published by Dr Davies of Liverpool University [8]. Improvements to the scheme could be made by eliminating the heat losing solar walls on the west and north, providing movable insulation to the south solar wall (Morgan proposed electrically operated shutters in his patent), ensuring minimal ventilation in winter yet adequate cross ventilation in summer, and providing external blinds or overhangs for summer protection.

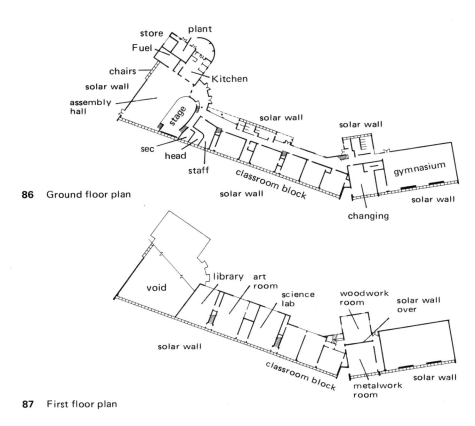

86 Ground floor plan

store
plant
Fuel
chairs
solar wall
assembly hall
Kitchen
stage
solar wall
solar wall
sec
head
staff
classroom block
solar wall
gymnasium
solar wall
changing

87 First floor plan

void
library
art room
science lab
woodwork room
solar wall over
solar wall
classroom block
metalwork room
solar wall

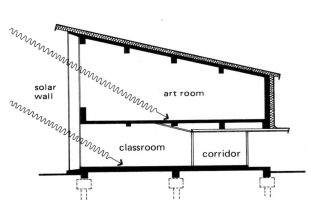

88 Section

solar wall
art room
classroom
corridor

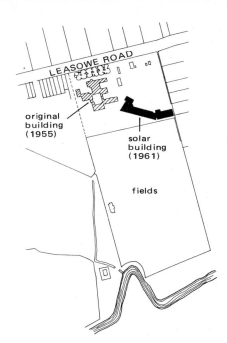

89 Site plan

LEASOWE ROAD
original building (1955)
solar building (1961)
fields

90 South facing solar walls; note clerestory solar wall to woodwork room

Catalogue

SUMMERS HOUSE ✳

Address:	3 North Several, Blackheath, London SE3
Architect:	Royston Summers
Solar engineer:	Arthur Aldersey-Williams
Date occupied:	September 1968

In 1965, architect Royston Summers got together with six other friends to develop a narrow wedge of land that lay on the south side of the Blackheath. The main axis of the land was east-west and afforded an opportunity to employ direct gain heating methods. Each of three storey, five bedroom homes has an area of 156 m^2 and was built at four-fifths the cost of low cost housing at the time. The overall dimensions of each house is 11.2 m by 6.7 m, remarkably similar to the plan outline of the Curtis house.

ENERGY CONSERVATION

The building's structural, thermal and acoustic properties were all optimised with the aid of a computer. The party walls are 250 mm double leaf construction with a sand filled cavity (U-value of 1.45 W/m^2°C). The window walls to the north and south are all factory sealed double glazing (U-value of 3.5 W/m^2°C) with curtaining used for movable insulation. The floors are made up of a 230 mm hollow pot slab (to facilitate service runs), 25 mm expanded polyurethane, and a 90 mm sand cement screed carrying the 24 kW underfloor, off-peak, electric heating system. (U-value of 0.55 W/m^2°C). The roof employs the same hollow pot structure but has 75 mm of insulation with a graded screed and felt roof (U-value of 0.27 W/m^2°C). The building is temperature zoned by level, but not in plan. The entry and large amounts of glazing are recessed and protected from the wind, while the top of the stair can be opened to permit it to act as a summer cooling shaft. The peak heat loss rate has been calculated at 12 kW.

PASSIVE HEATING

Direct gain heating is employed. The building is orientated 28° west of south, and the 49 m^2 of south facing glazing represents 32% of the floor area. Dark floor and wall tiles in the kitchen provide thermal storage, but in the dining room and upstairs bedrooms light coloured surfaces make the energy available for immediate use. Movable insulation is provided by curtains. The first floor balcony enjoys an unusually high standard of thermal comfort by being well-sheltered and lined with dark tiles that provide radiant heating.

PERFORMANCE

No monitoring has occurred but it is estimated by the designer that the house is 15—20% solar heated. Performance could be improved by providing better movable insulation behind the south facing glazing, greatly reducing the north facing glazing (incorporated because of the expansive view towards the heath) and providing external blinds or overhangs for summer protection.

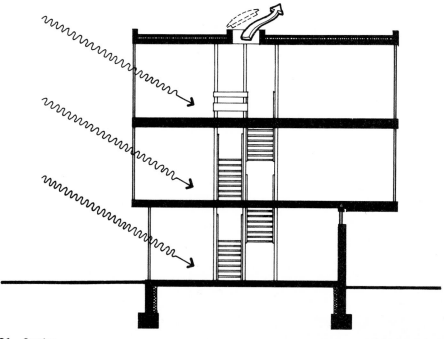

91 Section

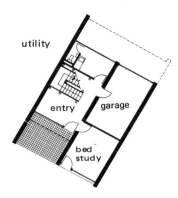

92 Ground floor plan

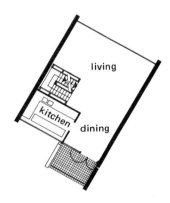

93 First floor plan

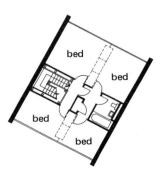

94 Second floor plan

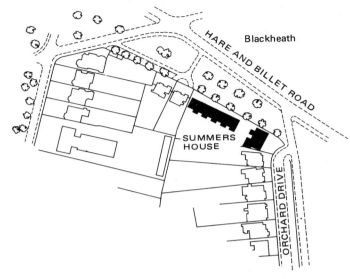

95 Site plan

96 South elevation showing large collector area

Catalogue

THAME FARMHOUSE

Address: Thame, Oxfordshire
Architect: Dominic Michaelis
Solar engineer: Dominic Michaelis
Date occupied: June 1970

In order to provide accommodation for the newly appointed head cowman, the owners of this Oxfordshire farm commissioned architect Dominic Michaelis to design a three bedroom house with attached garage. Apart from being easy to maintain and cheap to heat, the new building had to be built quickly and cheaply. Michaelis responded with a single storey steel framed structure that was built off a concrete slab. The building has an area of 113 m^2 and was completed in sixteen weeks at a cost of £7200.

ENERGY CONSERVATION

The protective walls to the north are cavity construction, the external leaf being brick-work and the internal leaf being insulating concrete block (U-value of 1.1 W/m^2 ^{o}C). The large expanse of south facing glass is double glazed (U-value of 3.5 W/m^2 ^{o}C) and the felt covered roof is insulated with 100 mm of woodwool (U-value of 0.76 W/m^2 ^{o}C). The plan is temperature zoned, with the living spaces to the south and circulation and service areas to the north. The enclosed entry acts as a draught lobby. The peak heat loss rate has been calculated at 8.5 kW, and the annual space heating load at 10,800 kWh.

PASSIVE HEATING

Direct gain heating is employed. The building was located so as to enjoy the view to the south, as well as to provide an unobstructed sun path. The large areas of south-east and south-west facing glass (equivalent to 25 m^2 of glazing facing due south) permit solar radiation to strike the black granolithic floor tiles and concrete block internal walls that act as thermal storage. Movable insulation is provided by heavy curtains. The collector area is 22% of the floor area. Auxiliary heating is provided by an oil-fired system (then an economical solution) that distributes heat from a finned oil-filled tube located in a plenum at the base of the windows.

PERFORMANCE

No monitoring has been undertaken, but the designer believes that the fuel bills are significantly lower than would have occurred in other building types and configurations under consideration at the time. Performance could be improved by providing better movable insulation and external blinds or overhangs for summer protection. The oil-fired auxiliary heating unit is currently being converted to a solid fuel unit.

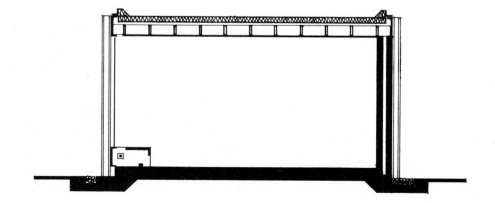

97 Section

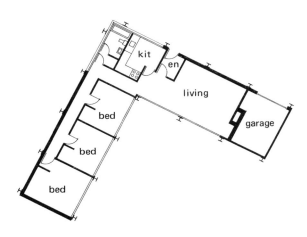

98 Plan

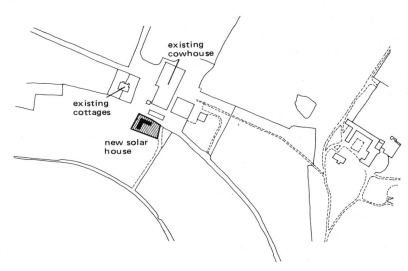

99 Site plan

100 View from south-east

Catalogue

STREET FARMHOUSE

Address: Kidbrooke Lane, Eltham, London SE9
Designer: Graham Caine
Date occupied: March 1973

The Street Farmhouse was the physical realisation of Graham Caine's belief that man should live in harmony with nature. The building itself was just one part of an integrated system that attempted to provide shelter, heat, food, water, cooking facilities and an ecologically sound waste disposal system for two people in an urban context. It can be directly compared to the Cambridge Autarkic House project that began at much the same time, but with a much larger budget when compared to Caine's initial £200. While still a fifth year Architectural Association student, Caine obtained a two year planning permit to erect the two storey, 70 m^2 timber framed house on a sports field in Eltham owned by Thames Polytechnic. The house was completed and occupied by Caine in March 1973. Occupation continued until August 1975 when the house was dismantled, after a year's extension to the planning permission had run out.

ENERGY CONSERVATION

The external walls consist of 100 mm square posts at 900 mm centres, clad externally with diagonal shiplapped boarding and internally with 500 mm thick woodwool sheets (U-value of 1.0 W/m^2°C). The ground floor was brickpaved or exposed earth. The first floor was T & G flooring on joists with mineral wool insulation, and the roof consisted of timber joists lined internally with T & G boarding, 150 mm mineral wool, 50 mm woodwool slab and covered with two layers of roofing felt (U-value of 0.2 W/m^2°C. The roof leaked, however, and had to be covered with polythene and a 50 mm layer of earth ballast. The building was temperature zoned and provided with a draught lobby.

PASSIVE HEATING

Solar greenhouse heating was employed. The attached greenhouse was 88 m^2 in plan area, and had a surface area of 135 m². It was nearly semi-circular and faced south. The timber framing was covered with two layers of polythene, kept apart by insulating spacers. The first floor living space could be heated with oxygenated warm air vented in from the greenhouse, and an openable flap at the top of the greenhouse could vent excessively hot air to the outside. Auxiliary heating to the living space was provided by a paraffin heater.

THE INTEGRATED SYSTEM

Domestic hot water was provided by three vertical, black painted panel radiators (total area 8.4 m^2) glazed with two layers of polythene. This thermosphoned directly into an insulated 225 litre water cylinder. Rainwater was collected off the greenhouse roof, passed through a sand filter and then used, with any excess being diverted to a butyl rubber lined pool, where goldfish, terrapins and skate swam. Sewerage was treated in a series of digestors that were designed to provide methane gas and effluent fertiliser.

PERFORMANCE

No systematic monitoring occurred, but the food cultivation, effluent fertiliser production, solar water heating and rainwater treatment were all considered to be successful. However the methane production and electricity generation were not. The solar greenhouse provided sufficient heat during the winter of 1972/73, that only 14 litres of paraffin oil were used for auxiliary heating.

Caine is carrying on his life style in a new but similar development at Thamesmead.

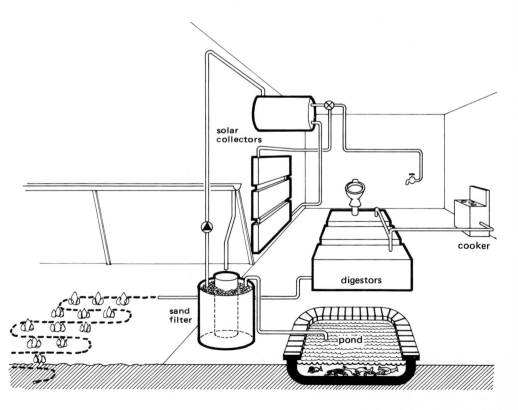

101 Integrated system

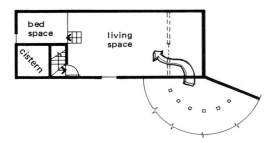

102 First floor plan

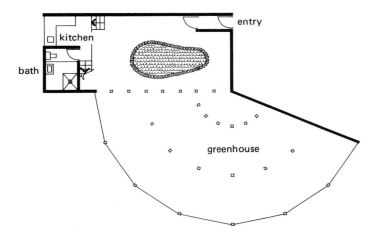

103 Ground floor plan

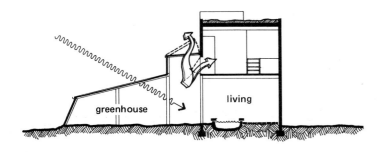

104 Section

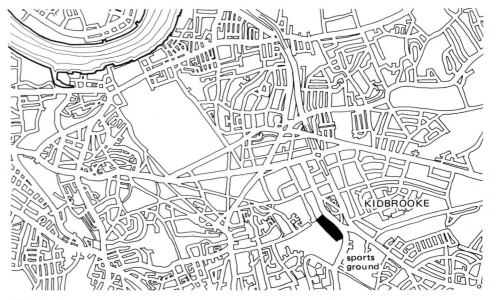

105 Site plan

106 South elevation

Catalogue

DELTA

Address:	The Street, Charsfield, Suffolk
Architect:	Cedric Green
Solar engineer:	Cedric Green
Date occupied:	September 1974

Architect Cedric Green built "Delta" to test the hypothesis that the most efficient space heating system for a whole building was to integrate the solar collector and thermal store into the actual building itself, eliminating the need for sub-systems. Aware of the performance of historical precendents (the 19th century conservatory and the glass clad office blocks typical of the early 1960's) Green incorporated thermal storage in the mass concrete floor to even out day and night-time temperature swing. Blinds and curtaining were used to control solar radiation and prevent summer overheating. Originally it was intended to be an owner-built structure, with just the central brick core erected by a contractor and then used later as a site hut by the owner. However, the two storey, three bedroom, 96 m² house was completed almost in toto by the builder, at a cost of only £11,000. This reflects the cost benefits to be derived from an owner-built programme.

ENERGY CONSERVATION

The prefabricated, Columbian pine structural frame is clad externally with a vapour barrier and 18 mm timber boarding, and internally with another vapour barrier and 12 mm boarding or foil-backed plasterboard. The cavity is filled with 100 mm glass fibre insulation (U-value of 0.25 to 0.36 W/m²°C). The roof has a similar construction and U-values, except that the timber boarding is replaced by timber shingles and roof felt. The concrete floor slab is insulated below with a pea-shingle hardcore (25 mm to 50 mm diameter) that has very low thermal conductivity, because 30% of its volume is trapped air. Conduction can only occur at the small points where the shingles touch. This hardcore is blinded on the top with a fine gravel (a U-value of 1.2 W/m²°C is taken for a perimeter band 700 mm wide only). The windows are mostly single glazed (U-values of 2.5 to 8.0 W/m²°C depending on wind, sol/air temperatures, curtaining etc), with the fenestration in the north pitch of the roof being double glazed Velux units (U-values between 2 and 3 W/m²°C). The building is temperature zoned, and a draught lobby has now been added.

PASSIVE HEATING

Solar greenhouse heating is employed. The conservatory is 16 m² in plan area and faces 15° west of south. It is timber framed and glazed with 30 m² of 4 mm float glass at a pitch of 53°. Thermal storage is provided in the 6.6 m³ quarry tiled, mass concrete, ground floor. Warm air in the conservatory is naturally thermosyphoned through the house by opening doors at ground floor level and louvres at first floor level, with air returning via the open stairwell. Auxiliary heating is provided by electric off-peak underfloor storage heating (no gas was available to the site). The temperature is the concrete floor swings between 14°C and 25°C.

PERFORMANCE

Between January and April 1975, records kept at the house monitored daily temperatures, electricity consumption, weather conditions and significant activities and movements that might affect the thermal balance. When correlated on a computer with daily radiation levels, wind speeds, and sunshine hours taken from a nearby meteorological station, Green estimated that over the four month period the conservatory provided 5480 kWh of useful heating, representing 43% of the total space heating demand, assuming the conservatory is considered as usable living space (which it is). The house had the tendency to become unnecessarily warm upstairs during the day because of rising warm air, and too warm at night because of the heat stored in the slab; also during very sunny spring or autumn days the conservatory tended to overheat because the rate of heat transfer to the thermal storage was too low. These problems could be overcome by altering the location and size of the thermal storage, and by providing external overhangs or blinds to prevent summer overheating.

This elegant and cost effective example of passive solar heating was the germinating seed of work now being carried out by Green at Sheffield University. This work consists of the erection of a low energy structure (affectionately known as The Shed) that employs the same heating principle as Delta. This later work recently won third prize in the sixth Misawa Homes Design Competition in Japan.

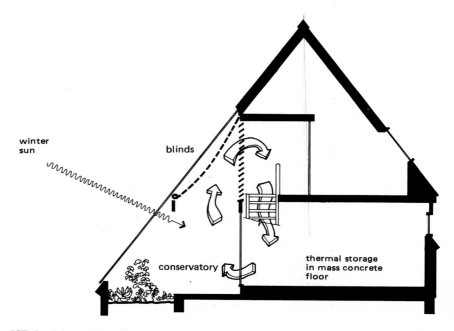

107 Section and solar diagram

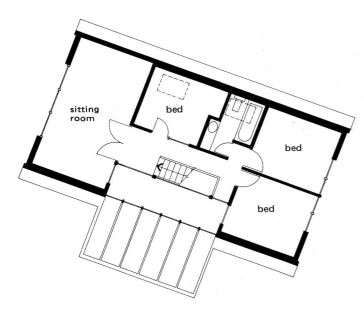

108 First floor plan

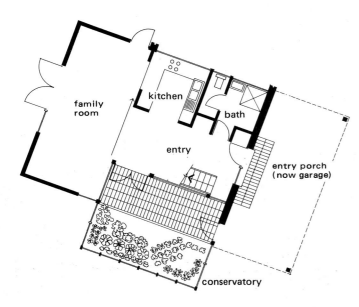

109 Ground floor plan

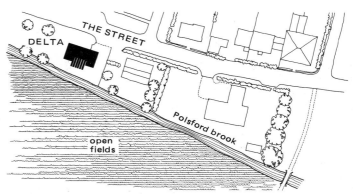

110 Site plan

111 East elevation showing double-height conservatory

Catalogue

MILTON KEYNES HOUSE

Address: No 3, Harrowden, Bradville, Milton Keynes
Architect: Milton Keynes Development Corporation Architects
Solar engineer: S. Szokolay, P. Artherton, D. Hodges
Date occupied: March 1975

After an initial feasibility study by S. V. Szokolay, who at the time was a senior lecturer at the Polytechnic of Central London, the Department of Energy gave a grant to the Polytechnic which, in collaboration with the Milton Keynes Development Corporation, selected a typical two storey, three bedroom 90 m² local authority house in the Bradville estate to demonstrate the feasibility of solar assisted space and water heating. A computer programme was written to simulate the performance of the system and a detailed monitoring procedure is being used to evaluate the performance of the system and consequently improve it, as well as to validate and modify the computer programme.

ENERGY CONSERVATION

The thermal properties of this solar house were intentionally not altered since the system, and not the house, was under test and the performance of the solar system could be directly related to other similar, but traditionally heated, houses on the estate. The house was built to Parker Morris standards and the then current Building Regulations insulation standards. The external walls are timber framed, clad with asbestos cement sheets and provided with 25 mm of glass fibre insulation (U-value of 0.75 W/m²°C). The timber framed roof is clad with tiles (U-value of 0.55 W/m²°C). Windows are single glazed. The peak heat loss rate has been calculated at 6.7 kW and the annual space heating load at 6750 kWh.

PASSIVE HEATING

Unintentionally, direct gain heating is employed. The living room windows face 10° east of south and provide 10m² of collector area. The 100 mm thick concrete floor acts as thermal storage. Movable insulation is provided by curtains.

ACTIVE HEATING

A liquid flat plate collector system is used. Eighteen Alcoa roll-bond aluminium panels were fixed to the top of the rafters (at a pitch of 34° and at an orientation of 10° east of south) and weatherproofed by traditional patent glazing fixed at 969 mm centres. Glazing was of 4 mm low iron content single glass sheets. The 34.5 m² of effective absorber area (compared to 37 m² of metal collector) were insulated at the back with 100 mm of glass fibre. A water/17% glycol solution is pumped through the collectors to the thermal store that consists of two large rectangular steel tanks (one each on the ground and first floors) that hold a total of 4200 litres of water. The tanks are insulated with 100 mm of glass fibre and are sized to store two days heat in October and March. Solar heated water is pumped to a modified space heating fan convector unit, with alternative heating provided by a 6.5 kW input gas fired boiler. Domestic hot water is preheated by having it pass through a series of internal preheaters located within the thermal store, then onto a 250 litre traditional hot water cylinder that has a 3 kW electric immersion auxiliary heater.

PERFORMANCE

The system initially performed very badly with only a 17% contribution to the space heating load and 57% to the domestic hot water load. Recent modifications, however, have dramatically improved these performances. The collectors have been sprayed with a high absorptivity matt black paint (Nextel Velvet Coating by 3M UK Ltd). The space heating control was altered to include a two stage thermostat that makes allowance for separate gas and solar heating modes (thus making better use of low grade heat). More insulation was added to the domestic hot water cylinder which, combined with a lower thermostat setting, reduced the amount of auxiliary energy required. In addition the fan in the space heater was changed from 500 W to 200 W, and more antifreeze was added to the circuit (thus reduced the amount of night-time cycling required to prevent freezing). These changes have resulted in a 37% contribution to the space heating load and a 70% contribution to the domestic hot water load, giving an overall contribution of 47%. These results tie in well with the present improved computer model.

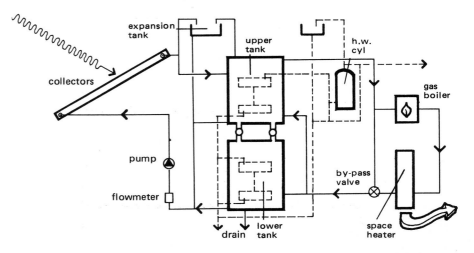

112 Solar system

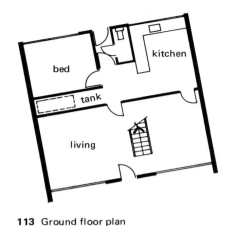

113 Ground floor plan

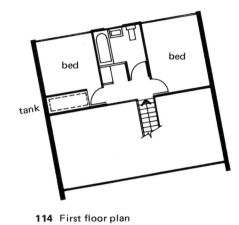

114 First floor plan

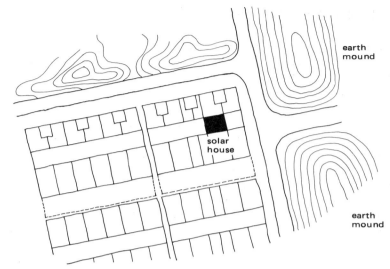

115 Site plan

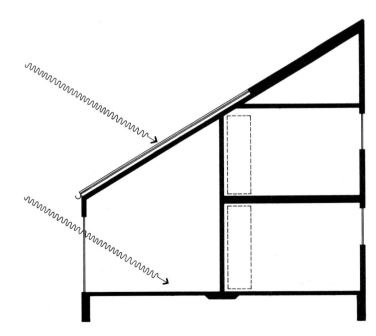

116 Section

117 View from south-east

Catalogue

ANGLESEY HOUSE

Address: The Drive, Malltraeth, Anglesey, Wales
Architect: David Bonnett
Solar engineer: S. Szokolay
Date occupied: April 1975

During preparation on an Open University course on physical resources, geologist J. B. Wright became interested in the applications of solar energy and made contact with Steven Szooklay, who was then involved in planning the Milton Keynes House. Szokolay agreed to help instal a space and water heating solar system in a bungalow that the Wrights planned to build at Malltraeth. Working chiefly with Bridget Wright (and the architect), he made modifications to the plan, orientating the building due south and designing and detailing the solar system. The result was a 95 m^2 single storey house (80 m^2 of which is heated) with a volume of 325 m^2 (270 m^3 of which is heated). It is the first provately built, liquid flat plate collector, solar space heating system in Britain.

ENERGY CONSERVATION
The load bearing brick/block walls have cavity fill insulation (U-value of 0.48 W/m^2 $^\circ$C). Around the perimeter of the concrete floor, a 900 mm width of 50 mm thick polystyrene insulation is located below the slab and turned up at the edge in a 25 mm thickness (U-value of 0.61 W/m^2 $^\circ$C). The concrete tile roof was lined internally with T & G boarding, and filled with 100 mm thick polystyrene blocks (U-value of 0.58 W/m^2 $^\circ$C). All windows are double glazed. The calculated peak heat loss rate is 5 kW.

PASSIVE HEATING
Direct gain heating is employed. The south facing living room windows have an area of 11 m^2, and thermal storage is provided by the dark brown quarry tiles set on the concrete floor, as well as the internal concrete block partitions. A conservatory was added in mid-1976, providing some additional heat to the adjoining bedroom and living room.

ACTIVE HEATING
A liquid flat plate collector system is used. Sixteen 2500 mm by 825 mm Alcoa roll-bond collectors (the same as those used at Milton Keynes) were fixed on top of the 30° pitched rafters to provide an effective absorber area of 33 m^2. Horticultural glass (8 mm) was initially fixed between the patent glazing bars (at 1220 mm centres) but later replaced by 6 mm St. Gobain low iron content glass in all but two sections. The collectors were connected to a 2550 l. storage tank (900 x 900 x 3050 mm high) made of 6 mm mild steel, and the heat distributed to the house via four independent under-floor circuits consisting of a total of 340 m of 10 mm cpooer tubing imbedded in the 32 mm floor screed at roughly 230 mm centres. This heated floor can use water with a temperature as low as 25°C in mid winter, while in summer it can act as a thermal "overflow" for excess heat. Auxiliary heat is provided by electric immersion heaters (two 3 kW units for the space heating tank and one 2.3 kW unit for the domestic hot water), a wood burning stove that is also used for cooking, and a portable 2 kW electric fan convector.

PERFORMANCE
No detailed monitoring has been done, but Wright has kept records of electrical consumption and rough estimates of wood burnt, and correlated these with records of sunshine hours measured at a RAF base 16 km away (11) (12). With those figures Wright suggests that the solar system provides about half of the space heating load, with a payback period of four to five yeats for the Anglesey location. Addition of the conservatory in mid-1976 was followed by a reduction in off-peak power consumption that was maintained till mid 1978. The passive heating performance would be improved by the use of better movable insulation, and external blind or overhangs to prevent summer overheating. The active system could be improved by the Incorporation of a heat exchanger on the collector circuit to reduce the amount of anti-freeze required, the elimination of different metal types (aluminium, steel, copper) in the fluid system, and an easier method of glass removal for collector maintenance and repair.

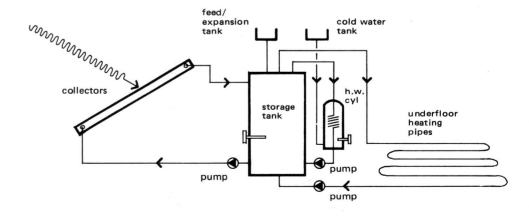

118 Solar system

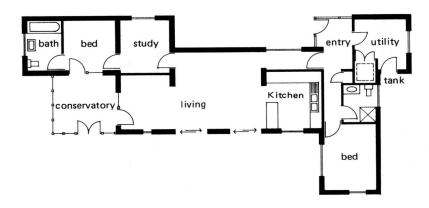

119 Plan

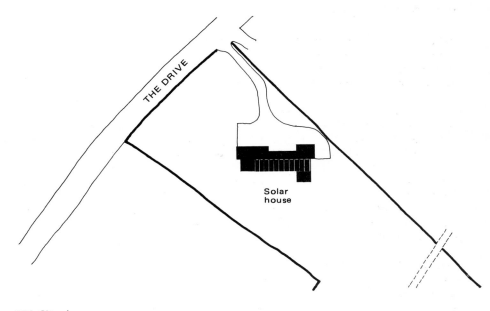

121 Site plan

THE DRIVE

Solar
house

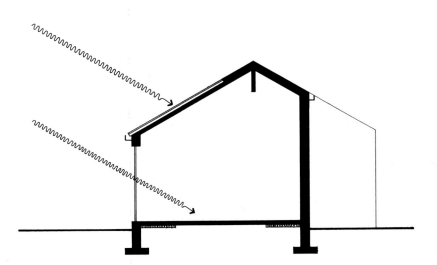

120 Section

122 View from south-east showing collectors and conservatory

67

Catalogue

FULMER LABORATORY

Address: Fulmer Research Institute, Hollybush, Stoke Poges, Buckinghamshire.
Architect: Solar Energy Developments
Solar engineer: Solar Energy Developments
Date occupied: April 1976

In 1975, the scientific advisor of the Calor Group Limited, Dr R. Swayne, commissioned the Fulmer Research Institute (an independent research group started in 1946 and specialising in metals and plastics research) to prepare a report. This report was to evaluate the potential of a solar "package" suitable for space and-water heating in the UK low to medium priced house bracket. Fulmer's report ascertained there was a potential market and recommended that testing facilities for prototype designs be built. Soon afterwards, Dr Swayne chanced to meet Dominic Michaelis of Solar Energy Developments (SED) who suggested that these testing facilities could be provided by a lightweight mobile structure, which by pivotting on rollers could experimentally determine the effects of different panel orientations, and by including three roof pitches (20°, 30°, 40°) could quantify the effects of various collector tilts. With funding provided by Calor, construction began in early 1976 and the building was occupied and the system commissioned by April the same year.

ENERGY CONSERVATION
The laboratory test rig was designed to simulate the thermal performance of a two storey, 82 m^2, 4/5 person, three bedroom semi-detached house built to Parker Morris standards. Such a house would have had a specific heat loss rate of 250 W/^{O}C if built to then current insulation standards; but in anticipation of more stringent mandatory insulation requirements the specific heat loss rate of the rig was reduced to 140 W/^{O}C. To achieve this, the steel framed building was clad in insulated steel walling on three sides (U-values varying between 0.58 and 0.62 W/m^2OC that simulated various housing conditions), an insulated timber floor (U-value of 0.31 W/m^2OC), a multi-pitched roof incorporating the solar panels (U-value of 0.27 W/m^2OC), and a south facing glazed screen with interchangable panels of single glazing (U-value of 5.4 W/m^2OC) and insulated cladding (U-value of 0.3 W/m^2OC). A draught lobby is provided and the building was occupied by the research team involved with the project.

ACTIVE HEATING
A liquid flat plate collector system is employed. Experience gained from the development of the solar system in the Milton Keynes house (a project headed by Steven Szokolay who was then a senior lecturer at the Polytechnic of Central London and subsequently a partner in SED) helped SED in developing a solar package. It consisted of collectors linked to a vertical thermal storage unit occupying a minimum of floor area, with all elements being sized so they could all pass through a standard sized door opening. The panel area was limited to the south facing roof area of a standard Parker Morris house (that varied between 35 and 60 m^2) and subsequently optimised on a

cost benefit basis at 36 m². With 54 m² of collector available on the test rig roof (using twenty-seven standard Alcoa panels) it was possible to test one full sized and one half sized system at the same time. The collector panels were fixed between standard aluminium patent glazing bars fixed at 900 mm centres and single glazed with 6 mm float plate glass. Once commissioned, this system was monitored for twelve months, modified and improved, then monitored for a further twelve months. Both the original and modified systems operated with a water based thermal storage system designed by SED, but since mid 1978 a third system incorporating a hybrid water and chemical based storage system has been installed and monitored. Heat is distributed from all storage systems by ducted warm air, with auxiliary heat being provided by a gas fired boiler. In addition, all systems are designed to preheat water for the domestic hot water system.

PERFORMANCE
Continuous monitoring has been carried out since April 1976, but to date no results have been published.

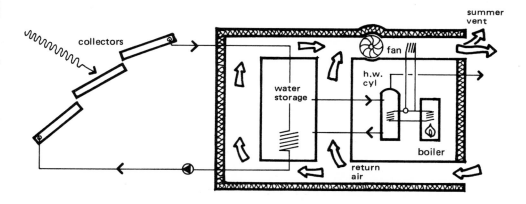

123 Solar system schematic

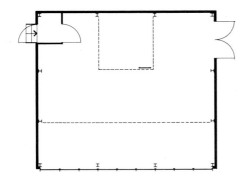

124 Ground floor plan

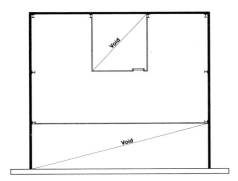

125 First floor plan

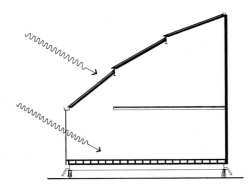

126 Section

127 Site plan

128 The laboratory structure showing collectors at three pitches.

Catalogue

MACCLESFIELD HOUSE

Address: Macclesfield, Cheshire
Architect: Don Wilson
Solar engineer: Don Wilson, Dr J C McVeigh, ECRC
Date occupied: May 1976

The concept of Granada Television's "House for the Future" was put forward by producer Brian Trueman in August 1974 and approved two days before Christmas the same year. The team that then gathered around Trueman consisted of architect Don Wilson, Dr J C McVeigh, the Electricity Council Research Centre (ECRC) Capenhurst and the prospective occupiers, the Grant family, who had been selected from 250 applicants. An existing two storey coach house on an 840 m^2 site was then selected by early 1975, and design work began on an intentionally overlarge number of solar heating options. It was felt that this wide range would afford the viewing audience a better chance of finding a solution relevant to their particular needs, rather than being presented with a single, predetermined panacea. A Do-It-Yourself (DIY) attitude was also promoted. The 125 m^2 four bedroom house was built mostly by the Grants during 1975 and 1976, and occupied by them in May 1976.

ENERGY CONSERVATION

The existing outer masonry walls were clad externally with 100 mm of insulation, then breather paper, then horizontal weatherboarding (U-value of 0.36 W/m^2 $^\circ$C). The new ground floor slab was continuously insulated below with 50 mm of polystyrene (U-value of 0.36 W/m^2 $^\circ$C), whilst the roof and solar collector were lined with 150 mm of glass fibre (U-value of 0.22 W/m^2 oC). The preferred window orientation was south-east or south-west. For other orientations where windows were required, they were restricted in area to the minimum Building Regulations allowance. All windows are double glazed, and all openings are weathersealed. A mechanical ventilation system is installed, and a heat exchanger recovers about 70% of the heat from the stale air being expelled. The house is temperature zoned, and the conservatory acts as a draught lobby. The peak heat loss rate has been estimated at 4.7 kW.

PASSIVE HEATING

Solar greenhouse heating is employed. The conservatory is attached to the south-west elevation of the house and is 30 m^2 in plan area. The 45 m^2 of glass roof is pitched at 27° and fixed to a timber structure. Heat can be delivered to the ground floor by opening the connecting doors, and to the first floor bedrooms by 100 mm flaps at the base of each bedroom window. Any excess heat can be stored in the 12 m^3 rock store located beneath the floor of the conservatory. This store is externally insulated with 50 mm of polystyrene.

ACTIVE HEATING

A liquid flat plate collector system is employed. The trickle type collector has an effective area of 42 m^2 (representing 34% of the floor area) and was installed on the south-west side of the roof at a pitch of 34°. A mobile gantry was installed to facilitate installation and maintenance. The collector is glazed with 4 mm horticultural glass, clipped and silicon sealed to the supporting horizontal glazing bars. The glass is butt jointed at the sides, and the 3 mm gap also silicon sealed. Thermal storage for the system is provided by three tanks containing a total of 5400 litres of water. A 1.5 kW heat pump transfers low grade heat from the 2000 litre dump tank (storing water below 25°C) to the 3000 litre space heating tank (operating between 25°C and 45°C). Heat is distributed by oversized thermostatically controlled radiators that operate at 25°C to 30°C. A 3.5 kW solid fuel boiler provides auxiliary heat via a 700 litre calorifier.

PERFORMANCE

The ECRC monitored the building between September 1977 and August 1978 [15]. It is estimated that passive solar heating provided 21% of the heat required, the heat pump another 7% and the flat plate collector a further 2%, totalling 30% in all. The passive contribution could be improved by the use of better movable insulation, and the active system contribution by a better control system and the use of more efficient collectors. The mechanical ventilation system has been very successful.

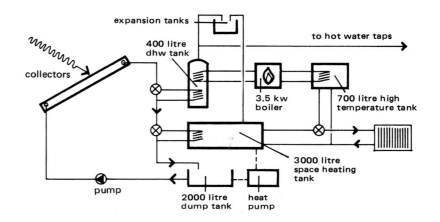

129 Solar system

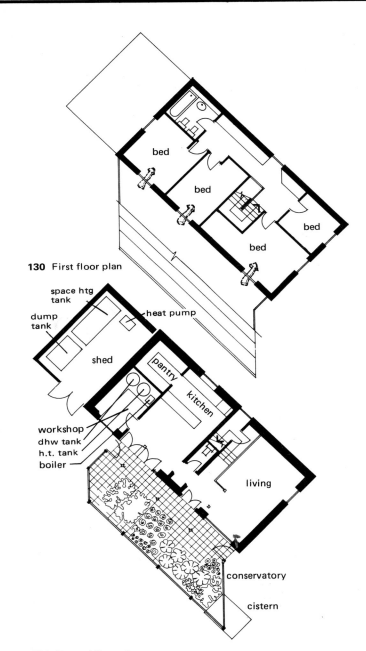

130 First floor plan

131 Ground floor plan

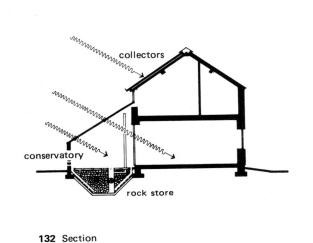

132 Section

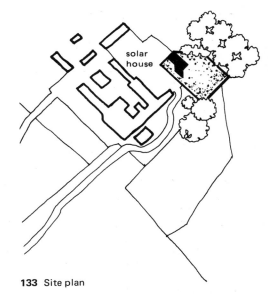

133 Site plan

134 View from west showing full length conservatory

Catalogue

NCAT EXHIBITION HALL

Address: NCAT, Llwyngwern Quarry, Machynlleth, Wales
Architect: R. James
Solar engineer: R. Todd
Date occupied: July 1976

Annually forty thousand people visit the National Centre for Alternative Technology (NCAT) that has been established in the Llwyngwern slate quarry, three miles north of Machynlleth, Wales. Quarrying ceased in 1952 and the site was abandoned as a tip till 1975. Since then however the NCAT, sponsored in 1974 by the Society for Environment and subsequently sustained by company donations and visitor's entrance fees, has established and maintained an outdoor display and demonstration project. These illustrate how "people can live happily on limited material resources, producing a minimum of waste and pollution, but without returning to the hardships of the past." The working hub of the Centre is an old two-storey slate-walled workshop that has been converted to an exhibition hall and bookshop on the ground floor (110m²), with offices and storage above (90m²). It was occupied in the summer of 1976.

ENERGY CONSERVATION

The original external walls of the building were slate. Within this perimeter structure, a 100 mm leaf of insulating concrete block was constructed, creating a 200 mm cavity. This cavity was partially filled with 150 mm of polystyrene insulation (total U-value of 0.2 W/m² °C). Any condensed vapour or rain penetration discharges down the inside face of the slate wall and drains out via 25 mm pipes at the base of the wall. The roof is insulated with 150 mm of self-extinguishing polyurethane (U-value of 0.19 W/m² °C) while the 65 mm ground floor screed is separated from the 100 mm concrete floor slab by 150 mm of polystyrene (U-value of 0.2 W/m² °C). Natural lighting has been maximised and the 50m² of double glazing in the east wall is partially fitted with insulating shutters of 40 mm translucent Okalux. Careful weatherproofing aims to achieve a ventilation rate of about one half an air change per hour. All these measures reduce the specific heat loss rate to 250 W/°C.

ACTIVE HEATING

A liquid flat plate collector system is used. It consists of 90m² of trickle type collector in two banks; 71.76m² at a 34° slope for summer collection and 26.4m² at 55° for winter collection. The water flow rate is 0.52 litres/sec. The collector consists of double glazing (two sheets of 4mm glass in 1920 by 580 mm sheets) fixed to standard glazing bars at 600 mm centres. The glazing bars are bolted to the timber roof purlins below, with the absorber plate being standard aluminium roof decking also fixed to the purlins. The decking is insulated at the back by 150 mm polyisocyanurate blocks, with a 22 mm air gap between for summer venting. The heating system attempts year round heating with no auxiliary input. Thermal storage is provided by a half-buried 100m³ interseasonal water store, located just in front of the collectors. Heat is distributed to the building via 10 mm nylon pipes embedded at 200 mm centres in the 100m² of sand/cement ground floor screed. This creates a large low temperature radiator panel that operates between 18°C and 25°C, with air temperatures at about 15.5°C. Auxiliary heat is provided by a wood burning stove.

PERFORMANCE

Twelve temperature points have been monitored, and between February and November 1978, the internal air design temperature of 15.5°C was maintained by the system, but between December 1978 and February 1979 auxiliary heating was provided by the wood burning stove. This resulted in the year-round maintenance of an acceptable comfort level, except for cold draughts experienced around the much used entry door and the base of east windows. The inability of the system to provide 100% of the space heating as intended is attributed to several factors; the connection of only the upper 71m² of collector, the low collector efficiency (due partly to condensation under certain weather conditions and the erosion of anodising on the panel around the high velocity inlet jets), the loss of water (caused by system leaks), some summer power failures and the absence of a throttling device at the outlet of the high temperature store that would prevent the surging of hot supply water into the heat distribution system. Modifications to rectify these faults are underway. NCAT are to be complimented on their efforts and their open attitude in the dissemination of information.

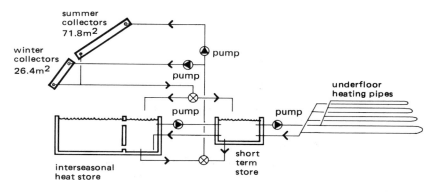

135 Solar system

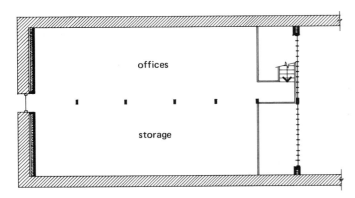

136 First floor plan

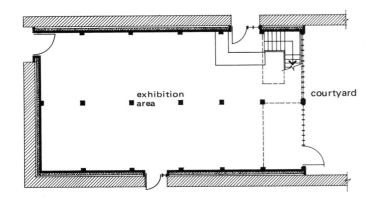

137 Ground floor plan

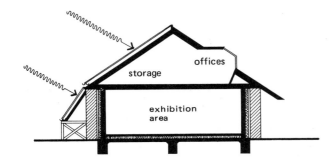

138 Section

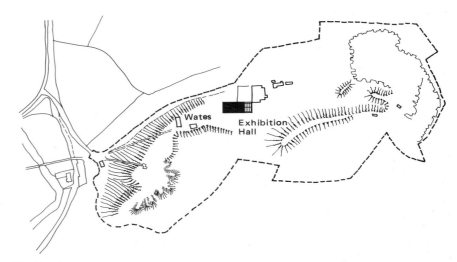

139 Site plan

140 The two arrays of collectors.

Catalogue

BLYTH HOUSE

Address: Blyth, Nottinghamshire
Architect: Design and Materials Ltd (D & M) staff architects
Solar engineer: D & M and Don Engineering Ltd
Date occupied: September 1976

The Worksop firm of Design and Materials Ltd offer a package deal service of drawings and structural shell materials for a wide variety of traditionally built houses and bungalows. In 1975 it decided to demonstrate how a solar heating installation could be incorporated properly and neatly into one of their popular standard house designs. The five plot development at Blyth was selected. It is close to a Norman Church, and Bassetlaw District Council demanded an unobtrusive solar installation. The two storey 154 m^2 four bedroom house was to be sold on the open market so it had to comply with the Building Regulations, qualify for a National House Building Council certificate, and be approved for a mortgage. Several other similar systems have been built and sold, but Design and Materials Ltd have now withdrawn the house from their range.

ENERGY CONSERVATION
The external walls were constructed in brick for the outer leaf and insulating concrete block for the inner leaf (U-value of 1.0 W/m^2 ^{O}C). The 100 mm ground floor slab has a 37 mm screed, but no insulation. The roof insulation level was increased by adding a 75 mm layer of insulation to the standard 50 mm insulating underslating felt (U-value of 0.4 W/m^{2O}C). All the windows were double glazed. The heak heat loss rate has been estimated at 10 kW.

ACTIVE HEATING
A liquid flat plate collector system is employed. Two banks of selectively surfaced absorber panel are used; 28.6m^2 on the main roof and 11.4m^2 on the garage roof, making 40m^2 in all. This panel area represents 26% of the floor area. The absorber panels are set between the rafters (located at 600 mm centres and pitched at 22½^O) and insulated at the back with 50 mm of closed cell low density polystyrene. Four lengths of 5 mm single glazing cover the 4 metre long absorber plates and are secured to the rafters with silicon rubber sealant set into rebates for easy replacement. (The proximity of the local cricket pitch made this consideration necessary). The collector array is orientated 40° west of south. Thermal storage for the system is provided by a heavily insulated 4000 litre externally located water container, as well as by the 340 litre hot water cylinder. Heat is distributed by a traditional ducted warm air system, that uses a 15 kW fan convector to warm the circulating room air. Heat for the convector is drawn for the main storage tank. This tank in turn is heated either by solar energy or by a 17 kW oil-fired boiler linked into the domestic hot water tank.

PERFORMANCE
Sheffield University monitored the installation for the two weeks prior to occupation [16], but equipment malfunction gave only seven days of reliable data. No system performance was evaluated, only collector efficiency, and it was concluded that this efficiency related closely to a computer simulation. The performance of the system could have been improved by adopting a better orientation, by elimination of the over-shadowing on the garage roof panels, and by relocating the auxiliary heating input.

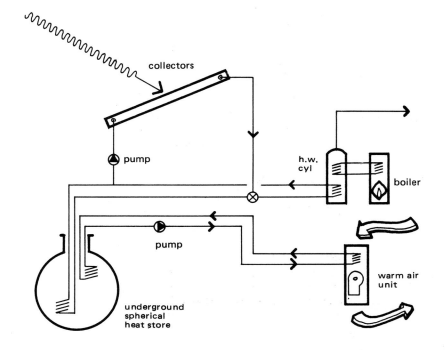

141 Solar system

142 First floor plan

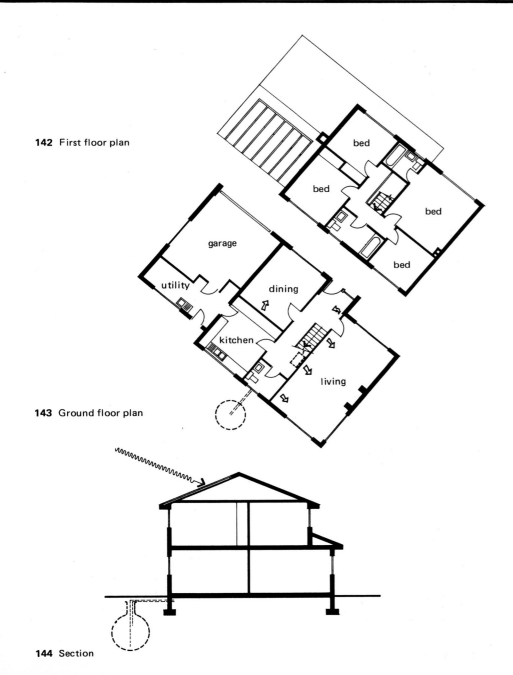

143 Ground floor plan

garage

utility

dining

kitchen

living

bed

bed

bed

bed

144 Section

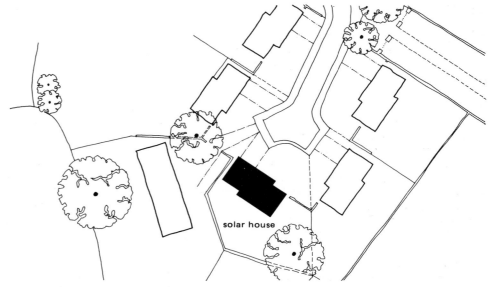

145 Site plan

solar house

146 View from south showing roof mounted collectors

Catalogue

WATES HOUSE

Address:	National Centre for Alternative Technology, Machynlleth, Wales
Architect:	Peter Bond Associates
Solar engineer:	Peter Bond Associates
Date occupied:	October 1976

In the summer of 1975, the National Centre for Alternative Technology (NCAT) approached Wates Built Homes Limited to take up the challenge of building a low energy house useing existing building technology. Wates agreed and commissioned Peter Bond Associates to design a 100m^2 two storey house with a conventional appearance, costing no more than £20,000 (which was achieved) and emphasising low energy demand (rather than alternative energy sources) so that the house would be applicable to any location. On its completion in June 1976, Wates donated the house to NCAT who opened it up for public viewing until September 1976. Occupation began after that.

ENERGY CONSERVATION

A massive 450 mm insulating blanket was wrapped around the entire house. The 700 mm thick walls consisted of a rendered 100 mm thick outer brick skin, 450 mm of "Dritherm" glass fibre insulation laid vertically in six 75 mm layers, with an inner skin of 150 mm thick Thermalite concrete block, returned at several places to buttress and tie the brickwork. This construction achieved a U-value of 0.075 W/m^2 $^{\circ}$C and a thermal time lag of 13 to 14 hours. Any condensation would drain down to weep holes at the base of the wall. The floor consisted of a concrete slab graded on the top towards the drainage holes in the outside walls; a layer of Netlon to support the 450 mm insulation 50 mm above the slab; a polythene vapour barrier; a 150 mm floor void that acted as a warm air supply plenum; and timber joists and flooring (U-value of 0.076 W/m^2 $^{\circ}$C). The roof consisted of a traditionally tiled pitched roof that is naturally ventilated; a polythene vapour barrier, and 450 mm of insulation that rests on a polythene vapour barrier backed plasterboard ceiling (U-value of 0.081 W/m^2 $^{\circ}$C). The windows are quadruple glazed with fixed outer double glazing 200 mm away from openable inner double glazing (U-value of 1.450 W/m^2 $^{\circ}$C). All these measures reduce the specific heat loss rate to 66 W/$^{\circ}$C, the peak heat loss rate to 1.2 kW, and the annual heating load to 950 kWh.

Other energy saving features include: a 275 litre waste water heat recovery tank coupled to the 180 litre hot water cylinder by a 0.18 kW heat pump; a cooking stove completely surrounded with 150 mm of insulation; a single entrance lobby with double doors; low wattage fluorescent lights; and a filtered rainwater system that provides all the water except that used for drinking purposes. All these measures mean that the building consumes only about ONE FIFTH of the energy of a similarly sized conventional house.

ACTIVE HEATING

A heat pump system is used. The unit consists of a 0.15 kW air/air heat pump (that uses the same type of compressor as a domestic freezer) with the evaporator placed in a stream of outside air (the heat source) and the condensor placed in a stream of recirculating room air (the heat sink). A c.o.p. of 2.5 is estimated. Fresh air is introduced at the rate of one quarter of an air change per hour and stale air is extracted from the kitchen and expelled over the evaporator to help prevent icing up in cold weather. The system can be reversed for summer cooling.

PERFORMANCE

A 24 input multichannel temperature recorder was installed by the architects in December 1976 but no firm results are available. The University of Sheffield are considering if they will now monitor the building. Wates, however, were impressed enough to commission the architects to design an 80m^2 two storey house on similar principles for sale on the open market at Croydon. Costing by Wates indicated that there was an increase in cost over the traditional house of only £2000 (roughly £1000 for the insulation and £1000 for the heat pump) with a payback period of about five years. Documentation was completed in 1977, but the houses were never built. This design approach, however, is very successful and should be vigourously pursued in the future.

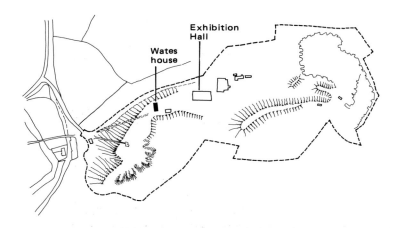

147 Site plan

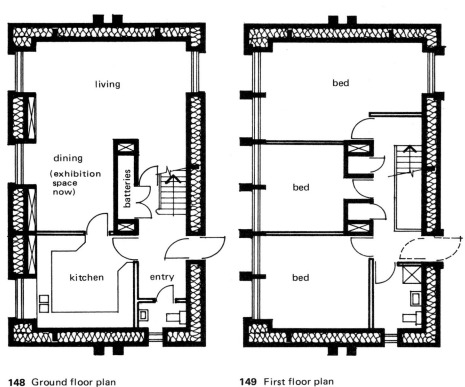

148 Ground floor plan

149 First floor plan

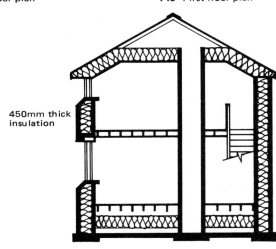

150 Section

450mm thick insulation

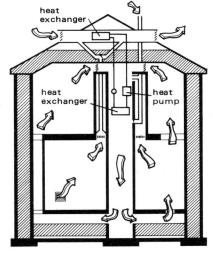

151 Winter operation

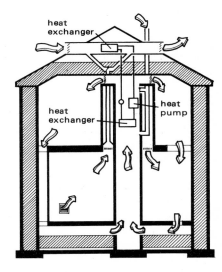

152 Summer operation

153 View from south-west indicating wall thickness by depth of window reveals

Catalogue

PLUMB HOUSE

Address: Castle Close, Great Leighs, Essex
Architect: Clive Plumb
Solar engineer: K.J. Harris
Date occupied: May 1977

As a personal extension of his work at the Basildon Development Corporation and involvement in energy conscious design, architect Clive Plumb built himself a 24m^2 four bedroom low energy bungalow at Great Leighs, Essex. The exposed site is wedged in between open land and the village cricket pitch. The "L" shaped single storey house is built like a stockade, with brick/block walls to the north (to shield off the cold prevailing winds) and a glazed screen to the south, providing a view of the garden and the sun. Normal services, except gas, were available to the site. The building cost £10,000, plus the owner's labour.

ENERGY CONSERVATION
The stockade walls are common brick externally, a 50 mm cavity, and internal leaf of 150 mm Durox insulating concrete blocks (U-value of 0.60 W/m^2 $^{\circ}$C); the end walls are 100 mm studwork lined with a moisture barrier and softwood boarding, lined internally with 9 mm plasterboard and insulated with 100 mm glass fibre mat (U-value of 0.60 W/m^2 $^{\circ}$C). The pitched tiled roof also has 100 mm glass fibre (U-value of 0.56 W/m²oC), and the 175 mm precast suspended floor slabs has a 38 mm screed (U-value of .57 w/m^2°C). The windows are single glazed. The house is temperature zoned and a draught lobby is provided. The peak heat loss rate is calculated by the designers at 8kW.

PASSIVE HEATING
Direct gain heating is employed. The south-west facing 15 m^2 glazing to the bedrooms represents 50% of the floor area. The glazing is angled at 70° to maximise collection, but still remain with the Building Regulations definition of a wall, rather than a roof. Thermal storage is provided by the concrete floor. Heavy curtains act as movable insulation.

ACTIVE HEATING
A solar assisted heat pump system is used. It provides heat for the domestic hot water and space heating systems. It consists of a 2.2kW input air/water heat pump which is hermetically sealed and totally immersed in 225 litre water tank and coupled to a 225 litre indirect hot water cylinder. The evaporator consists of a copper coil in the 1m^2 solar collector built behind the south facing glazing. Heat is not only transferred from the collector absorber plate but also from ducted warm air that has been heated in the roof space. Here the dark coloured roof tiles act as a low grade solar collector.

PERFORMANCE
No detailed monitoring has occurred, but by comparing thermal calculations and electricity consumption, Plumb estimates that direct gain satisfies about 30% of the heating load with the heat pump operating at an annual co-efficient of performance of 3. The passive contribution could be improved by better movable insulation, external blinds or overhangs to provide summer protection, and a more southerly orientation.

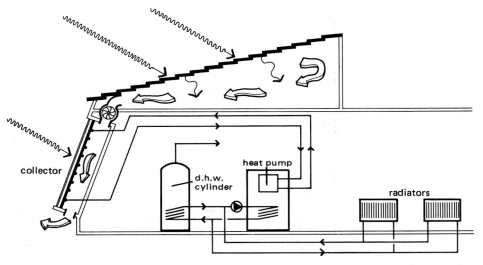

154 Solar system

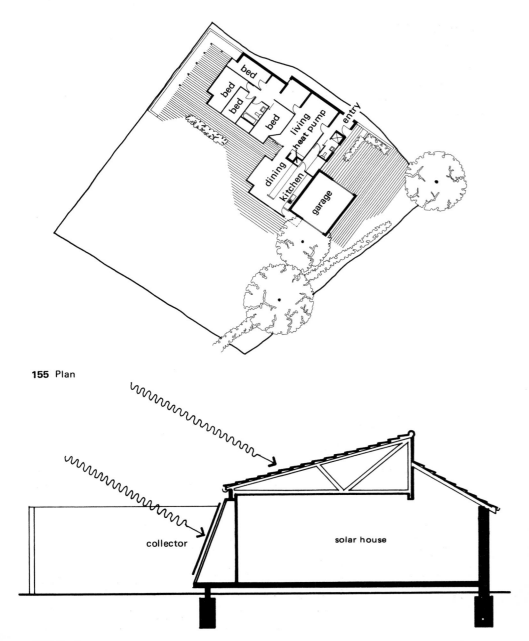

155 Plan

156 Section

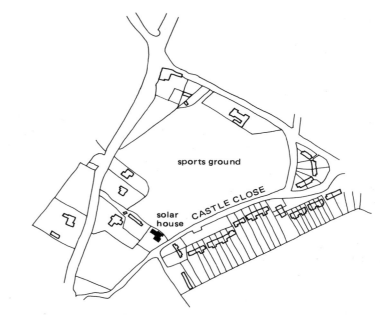

157 Site plan

158 View from west showing sloping solar collector

Catalogue

WILSON HOUSE

Address: near Basingstoke, Hampshire
Architect: the owner in conjunction with Guildford Design Group
Solar engineer: Helix Multi Professional Services
Date occupied: September 1976, system commissioned July 1977

Owner Brian Wilson was interested in incorporating an energy efficient heating system into his newly planned two storey, three bedroom home. He approached Lennox Industries Ltd in Basingstole for advice. He was directoed to Christopher Dodson who was involved with heat pumps, and told of a system that Dodson and architect Julian Keable had developed for Keable's own London house. Wilson agreed that this system would be suitable for his 130 m² house, and employed Helix Multi Professional Services (a company formed by Dodson and Keable) to carry out the consultancy. The heating system was costed at £1850 in 1975.

ENERGY CONSERVATION

The ground floor external walls are brick and insulated studwork (U-value of 0.26 W/m²°C) and the first floor walls are shingle clad insulated studwork. The 125mm concrete floor slab has a 38 mm screed (U-value of 0.57 W/m² °C). The timber truss roof is clad in concrete tiles and 150 mm fibre glass insulation rests on the plasterboard ceiling (U-value of 0.27 W/m² °C). All the windows are double glazed. The peak heat loss rate is calculated at 4.6kW under still wind conditions.

ACTIVE HEATING

A solar assisted heat pump system is employed. The design philosophy aims at optimising the efficiency of the heat pump. In order to reduce the difference in temperature between the heat source and the heat sink, the whole roof area (approximately 110 m² facing north-west and south-east and pitched at 25°) is used as solar collector to supply preheated air to the 10kW output air/water heat pump located in the attic. Air enters the roof at eave level via the collector channels formed by the underside of the roof tiles and a roof felt backing attached to the tile support structure. The air has a velocity of approximately 740 litres/sec for the whole roof area. This air is drawn over the evaporator of the heat pump then expelled outside. The heat extracted is transferred to 22,000 litres of water stored below the ground floor level in three large polypropylene bags, each approximately 600 mm deep. These rest on 50 mm of sand and are insulated with 50 mm of fibre glass (top) or polystyrene (sides). Removable timber hatches provide access. The thermal storage provided by these bags is sufficient to heat the house for 5 to 6 days, the computed maximum time for which the outside air is continuously below -1°C (when the heat pump efficiency drops markedly). Heat is distributed to the whole house by a ducted warm air system (a requirement since both occupants are heavy smokers and air cleaning equipment could be incorporated only with an air system). Air circulation is continuous, but at a variable speed, and once the demand for the house has been met, the speed drops to a minimum so that the normal effect of full on/full off cycling is not experienced.

PERFORMANCE

The system has been monitored since October 1977 by Dr. Neal of The University of Aston, Birmingham [17]. He estimates that the heat pump has a seasonal co-efficient of performance of 2.4, with the heat supply coming from three sources: ambient air (77%), solar energy (17.5%) and losses from the house to the attic (5.5%). The utilisation of the normal roof as a radiation absorber has been successful, and the provision of the thermal store has enabled the heat pump to operate at times when higher efficiencies can be achieved.

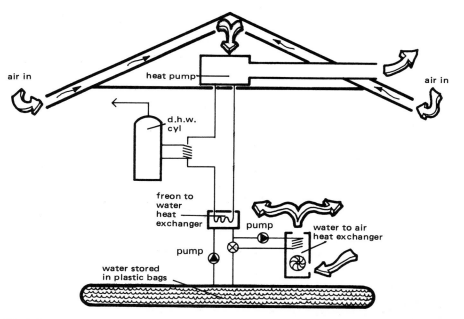

159 Solar system

160 First floor plan

161 Ground floor plan

thermal store below

utility

bed

bed

garage

heat pump in attic

gap at eaves

gap at eaves

thermal store (water in plastic bags)

162 Section

family

dining

kitchen

bed

living

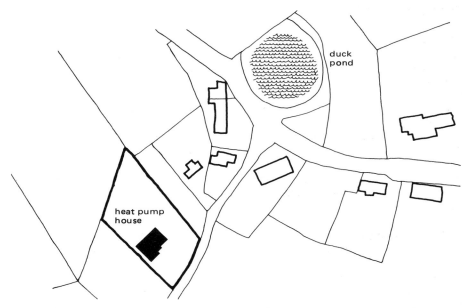

duck pond

heat pump house

163 Site plan

164 View from east showing air entry channels above gutter

SANDBACH COUNTY PRIMARY SCHOOL

Address: St. Peter's Rise, Elworth, Sandbach, Cheshire
Architect: Cheshire County Council Architect's Department (CCCAD)
Solar engineer: CCCAD and Shell's Thornton Research Centre.
Date occupied: September 1977.

To meet the extensive school buildings programme during the late 1960's and early 1970's, Cheshire County Council resorted to standard deep form plans for their primary school. The deep plan necessitated mechanical ventilation and this was provided by air-handling units located in the ceiling plenum. Air velocity was low, and heat was supplied by an oil-fired low pressure hot water unit. As a result of several monitoring exercises it was found that the control system required the boiler to cut in and out far too often (up to 15 times an hour). To eliminate this, a buffer was created between the heating load and the heating supply. This buffer was a 9000 litre water tank, now heated by a smaller boiler, sized to meet the average load rather than the peak load. By 1977 it was realized that the next logical step in this development process was the introduction of solar energy. In a politically favourable atmosphere, approval was given to build a small test installation at the Sandbach School, already under construction at the time. This single storey school was designed for 280 pupils and has a gross floor area of 1028m^2.

ENERGY CONSERVATION

The calculated U-values for the external brick walls are 0.42 W/m^2°C, the floor 0.32 W/m^2°C, the roof 0.52 W/m^2°C and for the single glazed windows 5.6 W/m^2°C. The irregular shaped plan has a draught lobby and controlled ventilation with heat recovery. The calculated peak heat loss rate is 140 kW.

ACTIVE HEATING

A liquid flat plate collector system is employed. A total area of 40m^2 of Alcoa aluminium panels are arranged in six planes, with pitches at 25° or 70° and orientations of south-east, south or south-west. The collectors are glazed with one layer of 4mm glass and set in patent glazing bars fixed at 600 mm centres. Thermal storage for the system is provided by a 4500 litre solar tank, that is made as tall as possible to encourage stratification. The primary circuit that transfers heat from the collectors to the thermal store uses an oil developed by Shell as the heat transfer fluid. The circulating piping was isolated from the aluminium collectors by specially developed rubber tubing. Heat is distributed within the school by air handling units, and two 30kW oil fired boilers provide the auxiliary heating. The cost of the solar equipment was £2500 and the associated building structure £3500.

PERFORMANCE

The system has been monitored, but the difficulty and time required to translate the information recorded into meaningful heat flows, has prevented positive results from being obtained to date. However, a computer model was constructed by the Thornton Research Centre. This forecasted that despite the small panel area (only 4% of the usable floor area) the solar system would satisfy approximately 7% of the annual heating and 21% of the domestic hot water load.

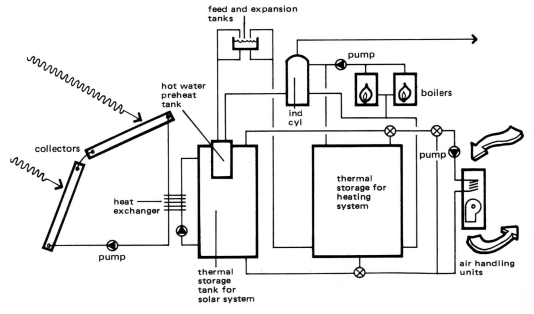

165 Solar system

166 Plan

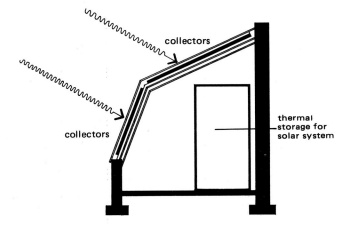

167 Section through plant room

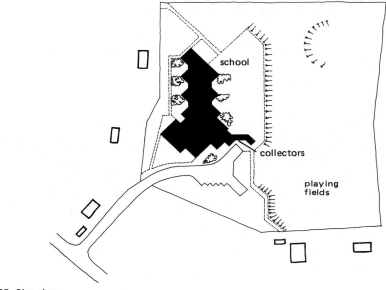

168 Site plan

169 View from south-east showing collectors on plant room roof

Catalogue

ROACH VALE COUNTY PRIMARY SCHOOL

Address: Roach Vale, Parsons Heath, Colchester, Essex
Architect: Essex County Architect's Department
Solar engineer: Essex County Architect's Department
Date occupied: September 1977.

Since 1971 the multi-professional architectural, engineering and research team of the Essex County Architect's Department have been promoting a long life/loose fit/low energy philosophy. The results of their approach is made manifest in an evolutionary series of buildings: Elmstead C.P. School (1973) which is a controlled environment gas heated building; Roach Vale C.P. School (1977) a controlled environment but heat pump heated building; Walton the Gunfleet (Tendring High) School (expected occupancy 1980) a controlled environment but solar assisted heat pump building; and Clacton St John Primary School (design stage only) a controlled environment, "in the ground" passive solar heated building. The process was begun in response to the post-war trend that produced elongated, structurally lightweight, thermally inefficient buildings with significant levels of occupant discomfort during the two extremes of the season, a situation created mainly by the mandatory imposition of the 2% minimum daylight factor.

ENERGY CONSERVATION
The integrated design, controlled environment approach pioneered at the 200 pupil Elmstead school was continued at the 280 pupil Roach Vale school.[19] The deep, square plan maximises the volume/surface area ratio. The sealed windows are restricted to only 17½% of the wall area (compared to 65% required by the 2% daylight factor) and supplemented by artificial lighting of about 300 lux. The building is artificially ventilated, with the heat pump providing a heat recovery facility. External doors have draught lobbies, and the medium weight modular component building system (M.C.B.) combines thermal insulation with a thermal time lag (approximately six hours). This dampens out excessive thermal changes. The walls in the MCB system are precast load bearing concrete panels (U-value of 1.26 $W/m^2{}^oC$). The floor is a concrete slab with precast concrete floor blocks (U-value of 0.3 $W/m^2{}^oC$) and the roof is precast lightweight autoclaved concrete, waterproofed with asphalt and covered with a 50 mm beach of pea shingle (U-value of 0.5 $W/m^2{}^oC$). The measures reduce the peak heat loss rate to 42.7 kW and the annual space heating load to 79,200 kWh.

ACTIVE HEATING
A heat pump system is employed. To heat the teaching block, four roof mounted Lennox air/air heat pump packages (with a total heat output of 14.5 kW) are grouped around the 52 m^2 central, glazed-roof courtyard. The heat source for the heat pumps is outside air, mixed in one case with warm but stale room air, that has been further heated in the glazed courtyard. (Room air is either recirculated or expelled to the outside via the courtyard or the toilets). The heat extracted from the air is transferred to the incoming supply air, that consists of a mixture of fresh air and recirculated room air. The warmed supply air is then ducted to the teaching areas by ceiling coffers. In summer, room temperatures are controlled by varying the rates of ventilation to the building and in extreme conditions, the heat pumps can be used to chill the incoming supply air.

PERFORMANCE
The Elmstead C.P. School was extensively monitored during the school year September 1974 to September 1975 by both the British Gas Corporation (R&D Division) and the Electricity Council, and it was found that the actual performance was significantly better than that predicted theoretically. At the Roach Vale C.P. School, monitoring is being carried out by the Electricity Council alone. Detailed measuring commenced during the school year 1979/1980 after a "settling in" period that allowed the school to approach its design level. Although no results are available, three general conclusions can be drawn: first, the external fabric of the building provides a six hour thermal time-lag; second, the warm air from the central courtyard reduces the heat pump operation time; and third, effective sealing of extract fans, roof mounted units and supply air coffers is required to prevent excessive loss of useful heat.

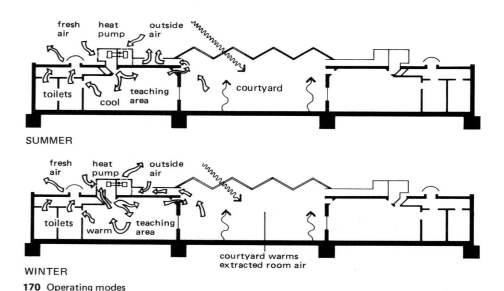

SUMMER

WINTER

170 Operating modes

171 Plan

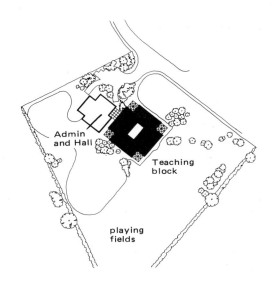

173 Site plan

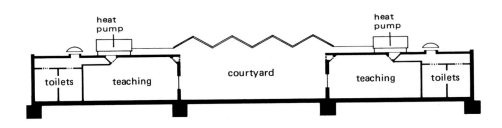

172 Section

174 View from north showing heat pumps on roof

INTEGRATED SOLAR DWELLING

Address: Brighton Polytechnic, Lewes Road, Moulsecoomb, Brighton, Sussex
Designer: John Shore and Frances Pulling
Date occupied: October 1977

The Integrated Solar Dwelling project goes back to 1969 when John Shore began research on ways to utilise ambient energy and recycled materials. His eventual aim was to produce an integrated, simple, low-cost building for two people, independently serviced so as to be self-sufficient in food, water, heat and light. Any by-products would be recycled within the building itself. A prototype dome was built and occupied in 1971, and two further designs were considered before the present design was adopted in 1973. After obtaining planning permission in 1976, construction was begun on land provided by the Brighton Polytechnic. The building was completed and occupied in October 1977 with funding being provided by the Polytechnic, interested companies and the designers. Shore's work can be compared to the Street Farmhouse and the Cambridge Autarkic Project.

ENERGY CONSERVATION

The $104m^2$ single storey timber framed building is divided into three elements. The first element is a $36m^2$ central living unit containing a living room/office, bathroom, kitchen and sitting room/bedroom that is used as a "cosy" area to retreat to in very cold weather. The walls, floor and ceiling are all insulated with 150 mm of pumped foam insulation that achieves a U-value of less than 0.2 W/m^2 $^{\circ}$C. Double glazed windows and doors are located on the south wall only, and 25 mm thick polystyrene shutters are erected at night for movable insulation. The second element is the 38 m^2 timber framed conservatory linked to the south side of the building by french doors. Glazing has been angled at 78° to maximise winter sun input and reflect a proportion of excess summer sun. The roof is pitched at 12°. Used both as living space and for food production, the conservatory acts as temperature buffer and wind protector for the south side of the living unit. The **third** element is the 30m^2 lean-to store on the north, that houses garden produce, bicycles, a food cool-store and a workshop; it also provides a temperature buffer and shield from northerly winds. Storage units at the east and west end of the living unit provide additional insulation. Initially 24 volt fluorescent lighting was installed but it was unsatisfactory and 240 volt mains supply lighting is now used. Ventilation is controlled via air vents located in the east and west walls, in the roof of the bathroom and in the insulated door in the north wall. These vents are also used for summer cooling. The peak heat loss rate for the 36m^2 living area is calculated at 700 watts and the annual space heating load at 673 kWh.

Rainwater is collected and stored in an external 4500 litre galvanised iron tank as well as three water tanks in the conservatory. Spray taps are used. An aerobic system of composting human by-products and vegetable trimmings is also employed. Since March 1978, a self-built 3.1m^2 solar panel is linked directly by a thermosyphoning circuit to a highly insulated 65 litre storage tank, providing pre-heated water for the domestic hot water system. A 150m^2 garden was laid out to the south of the building, and yields, cultivation time etc. were recorded. Shore proposed the garden in response to his concern that, while over 80% of the UK is farmland, it only provides 60% of the inhabitants' food requirements, and each week 400 hectares of farmland is converted to urban use.

PASSIVE HEATING

Solar greenhouse heating is used. The conservatory is 38m^2 in plan area and has an effective collector area of 40m^2. This represents 110% of the floor area. Thermal storage in the conservatory is provided by the earth, the plants and the water containers. The wall between the living spaces and the conservatory is 18% glazed, whilst another small section of the wall is built as a Trombe wall. Internal blinds in the conservatory act as a control to prevent overheating. Excessively hot air can be vented by removal of the eaves fillers at the edge of the corrugated plastic roof. Auxiliary heat is provided by a portable 1kW electric fan heater.

PERFORMANCE

The system has been monitored by the designers from November 1978 using two, six point chart recorders. To date no results have been published. In general, it appears that the "cosy" area is 13°C to 18°C warmer than the conservatory, which is generally 2°C to 5°C warmer than ambient. Sadly the project has recently been stopped by the Brighton Polytechnic, but the designers are intending to relocate the building on another site.

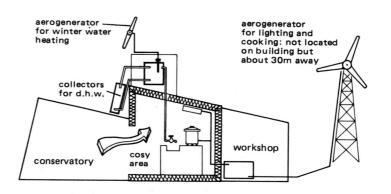

175 Solar system

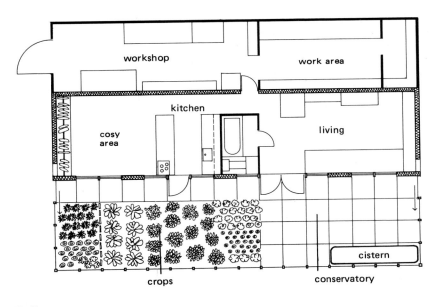

176 Plan

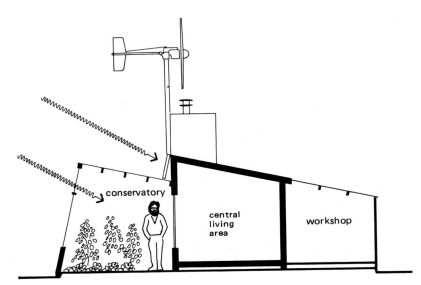

177 Section

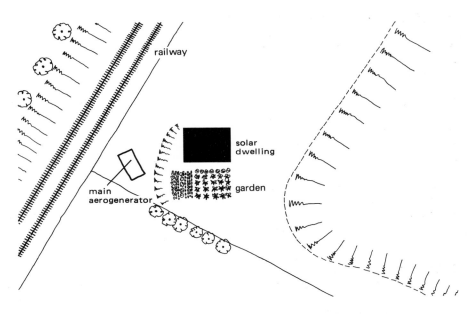

178 Site plan

179 View from west showing conservatory, solar collectors and aerogenerator.

Catalogue

PORT ISAAC COUNTY PRIMARY SCHOOL

Address: Mayfield Road, Port Isaac, Cornwall
Architect: Cornwall County Council, Architect's Department
Solar engineer: Hoare, Lea and Partners
Date occupied: May 1978

The new eighty place Junior and Infant Primary school at Port Isaac replaces the existing century old school that had previously served the village and its surrounding areas. Originally planned as an energy conservation project, the scheme was selected in June 1976 by the County Council in collaboration with the Department of Education and Science (DES) to be an experimental solar energy project. In September 1976, by working for three consecutive days in the seclusion of Bath University, members of the Council's Architect's and Education Departments, the DES and Hoare Lea and Partners produced the initial sketch scheme for the entire project. A prime consideration was to make the maximum use of solar energy without compromising the educational requirements of the school. What resulted was a 400 m² single storey building with three classroom units. A separate solar structure permitted the solar system to be easily maintained, or altered if need be, and allowed the school to be planned without compromise. Being an independent "package" the solar system could also find ready application to other buildings in the County, both old and new. Construction began in April 1977 and the building was completed in May 1978 for a cost of £95,000. The school is designed for 80 pupils.

ENERGY CONSERVATION

The building is traditionally constructed, but with a high level of thermal insulation: 50 mm styrofoam sheets are located on the inside face of the 100 mm wide cavity in the concrete block wall (U-value of 0.42 W/m²°C); 100 mm of fibre glass is located in the ceiling of the pitched roof (U-value of 0.31 W/m²°C) and a total of 125 mm insulation in two layers is built into the flat roof construction (U-value of 0.25 W/m²°C). The single glazed windows have been minimised in area and all have blinds or curtains to reduce heat loss in the winter and glare and heat gain in the summer. A draught lobby is provided. These measures reduce the peak heat loss rate to 16 kW, sixteen percent lower than the DES "Guideline" specification. The annual space and water heating load is 30,844 kWh.

ACTIVE HEATING

A liquid flat plate collector system is employed. The collectors are orientated due south with a total area of 92 m² built at two angles; 65° in the lower array to maximise winter collector and 35° in the upper array to maximise summer collection. The absorber panels are selectively surfaced with 3M Nextel. The collectors are single glazed with 4 mm float glass on the lower array and 6 mm float glass on the upper array. The glazing bars are at 582 mm centres with particular care being taken to minimise the height they project above the glass, in order to reduce

shadowing and wind turbulence effects. The collector area represents 23% of the usable floor area. The collector arrays are connected directly (i.e. with no heat exchanger) to two 5662 litre insulated, rectangular, mild steel water storage tanks. Provision is made for a third tank should it be required in the future. The connecting pipework is stainless steel. These tanks and the oil storage tank are located in the void below the solar collector panels. Water automatically circulates from the storage tanks to the collectors if there is any likelihood of damage from frost or overheating. Heat is distributed via a conventional central heating system using specially adapted fan and natural convector units, with supply/return water temperatures being at 38°C/33°C respectively. The solar system also provides heat for the domestic hot water system as well as a provision in summer months for a future trainer swimming pool. Auxiliary heating is provided by a 58 kW oil fired boiler (no gas was available to the site) that is linked to calorifiers in both the space and water heating systems.

PERFORMANCE

The building and system are to be monitored for two years by the University of Bath (Mr. G. Dane) with funding provided by the Department of Energy. A computer model will also be constructed. To date no results are available, though monitoring is expected to begin late 1979. It is estimated, however, that the annual saving in fuel oil could approach 30% for this school, rising to 50% if compared to a school of standard design.

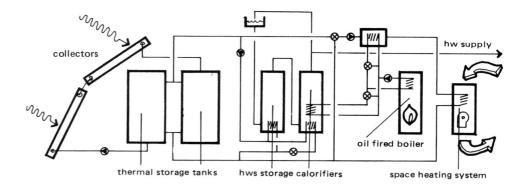

180 Solar system

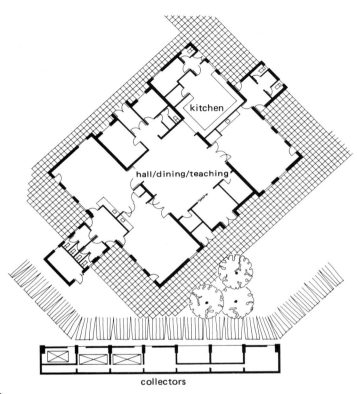

181 Plan

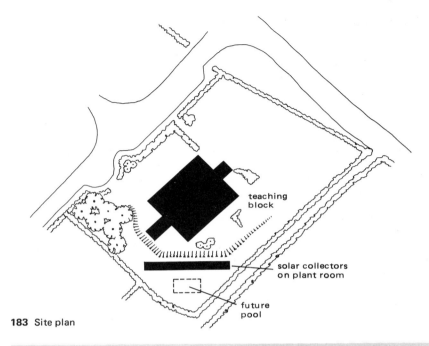

183 Site plan

teaching
block

solar collectors
on plant room

future
pool

kitchen

hall/dining/teaching

collectors

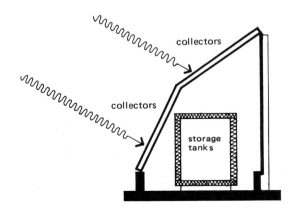

collectors

collectors

storage
tanks

182 Section through plant room

184 View from south-east showing the school behind the solar collector building

Catalogue

LIVINGSTON HOUSE

Address: 73 Camps Rigg, Knightsridge, Livingston, Scotland
Architect: Livingston Development Corporation
Solar engineer: P.P. Yaneske, University of Strathclyde
Date occupied: May 1978

Further to reports in August 1975 and January 1976 on the use of air and water as heat distribution mediums, P. Yaneske carried out a report on housing energy economics. He compared three different structures that were all based on a typical Livingston Development Corporation house type. The first structure was the typical house, and it was used as a reference point. The second structure was the same as the first but with a higher level of insulation, and the third structure was the same as the second except it now incorporated a heat pump heating system instead of the usual gas fired system. The Development Corporation had emphasised that since all houses were to be occupied by ordinary tenants, any new heating system had to be reliable, foolproof, unobtrusive, cost competitive and involve a minimum of specialist trades in the installation. Yaneske produced such a system. It was incorporated into No 73 Camps Rigg, a standard two storey, three bedroom, 96 m^2 house. The house next door was left unoccupied and used as a control.

ENERGY CONSERVATION
No special measures were taken and the house was constructed to the then current Building Regulation insulation standards. The walls are constructed with 250 mm of no-fines concrete, a 12 mm air gap, and lined internally with 10 mm plasterboard (U-value of 1.2 W/m^2°C). The floor is timber and has a sealed solum (U-value of 0.3 W/m^2°C). The roof is constructed with concrete tiles, 25 mm of fibreboard insulation, a loft space, 100 mm of blown cellulose insulation and 10 mm of plasterboard (U-value of 0.27 W/m^2°C). The windows are single glazed. The calculated peak heat loss rate is 6.4 kW and the annual heating load 20,800 kWh.

ACTIVE HEATING
A solar assisted heat pump system is used. Outside air is drawn in under the eaves and ducted up under two sections of the roof. These ducts are 5 metres long, and have a cross-section of 1000 mm by 100 mm. They are formed on the top by dark green concrete roof tiles lined with building paper, and on the bottom by foil backed bitumen paper. These ducts have a pitch of 26° and face due east , and a temperature rise of up to 3°C can be attained. Exiting from the collector at ridge level the air then passes into the attic space to collect any further gains available (i.e. heat loss from the house). This air is then drawn over the evaporator coil of the 1.7 kW input air/water heat pump before being discharged to the outside. The extracted heat is transferred to the condensor coil located at the head of the supply air duct. Auxiliary heating can be added to this supply air by electrical resistance coils. When heat is not required for space heating, a heat exchanger in the condensor circuit transfers heat to

a 300 litre domestic hot water cylinder. Heat for defrosting can be drawn back from this tank when and if required.

PERFORMANCE
Monitoring is being conducted by Yaneske, using a system that was commissioned in the middle of 1977. To date, two 10 day periods have been monitored in the winters of 1977/78 and 1978/79. A computer model has also been constructed for use in a validation exercise. An annual C.O.P. of 2 for the heat pump is predicted.

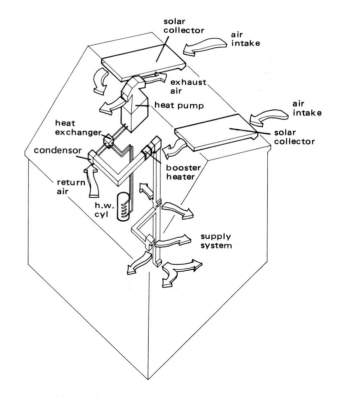

185 Solar system

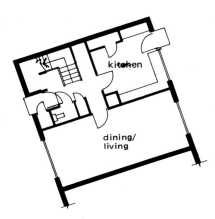

186 Ground floor plan

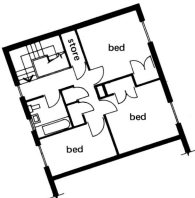

187 First floor plan

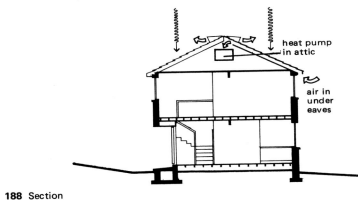

188 Section

heat pump
in attic

air in
under
eaves

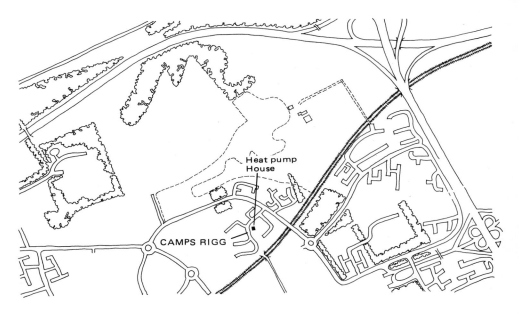

189 Site plan

Heat pump
House

CAMPS RIGG

190 View from north showing exhaust vent on roof

Catalogue

HIGHER BEBINGTON

Address:	Acorn Close, High Bebington, Wirral, Cheshire
Architect:	Paterson, Macauley and Owens
Environmental designers:	Peter Greenwood and Howard Ward
Date occupied:	July 1978

Just ten kilometres away from the Wallasey School, a second passive solar building has been completed on the Wirral. In 1973, architect Peter Greenwood and civil engineer Howard Ward (both then at Loughborough University of Technology) formulated the essential design principles involved. In 1974 they were appointed as consultants by the Merseyside Improved Houses (MIH) housing association. The MIH architects for the site selected, Paterson Macauley and Owens, responded readily to the idea of a new type of house that utilised solar energy. Once the basic design had been resolved, Pilkington Brothers Limited were brought in to provide technical support to assist in establishing estimates of the internal air temperatures. The final building consisted of fourteen, two person elderly people's houses, arranged in two terraces of five (one terrace solar heated) and two pairs of semi-detacheds (all solar heated). This Category I sheltered housing scheme was built for £190,000 and within Government cost yardsticks, using traditional materials and construction techniques.

ENERGY CONSERVATION

The 49 m^2 single storey dwellings are small but adequate and carefully considered. They are highly insulated: 100 mm of fibre glass in the walls (U-value of 0.29 W/m^2°C); 50 mm of fibre glass, resin bonded between the screed and the slab (U-value of 0.32 W/m^2°C) 100 mm of fibre glass on the ceiling and 80 mm of fibre glass roof board in the roof (combined U-value of 0.16 W/m^2°C); and all the windows are factory sealed double glazed units. These measures reduce the peak heat loss rate to 3.3 kW compared to 4.9 kW for the control houses, that were insulated to current Building Regulation standards.

PASSIVE HEATING

A thermal storage wall heating mode is employed. A 25 m^2 Trombe wall is constructed with dense, black bricks (2200 kg/m^3) that form the 225 mm thick wall, the thickness being determined by yardstick costs when considered in relation to performance (a 337 mm thick wall offered only marginally better thermal performance). Sealed double glazing is located 600 mm away from the face of the wall for ease of maintenance. The glazing is fixed into a timber framework thus creating the gap for room air to enter, become heated, rise and circulate back to the living spaces. Four separate metal ducts at ceiling level in the house link vents in the solar wall to the living room, kitchen and bedroom (two ducts). This ducting is necessitated by the double volume planning. Air in the attic (heated by the upper part of the Trombe wall) can be sucked into the bedroom ducts by fans, to provide additional heating in February/March and October/November. Loft space hatches are opened in this heating mode to allow free air circulation. This additional heating mode, however, is rarely used by the tenants. Auxiliary heating is provided by a 4.5 kW fan assisted off-peak storage heater in the lounge room that is linked into the air ducting system (a smaller unit would have been used if it had been available); a 0.75 kW infra-red wall heater in the bathroom; a 1.2 kW fan convector in the kitchen; and convector panel heaters in the bedroom (1.5 kW) and hall (0.5 kW). The kitchen, bedroom and hall units are controlled by time switches. Manual override is necessary for the use of any appliance outside the Economy 7 tariff.

Summer overheating is prevented by gaily coloured external blinds operated by winch handles. Natural circulation is promoted by venting the solar wall at the top, with living room and bedroom doors being louvred to assist air movement. The solar wall vents are linked to vents in the ceiling ductwork, so that only one set of vents can be open at one time. A multi-speed fan in the north wall provides any necessary boosting to air circulation.

PERFORMANCE

The cost of the extensive monitoring of both the solar and control houses is being shared between the Department of Energy and Pilkington Brothers Ltd. The monitoring team for the next two-year period consists of the designers, representatives from Merseyside Improved Houses, Pilkingtons and the Department of Energy. No results are available yet, but a computer model predicts a solar contribution of 30% to 60%.

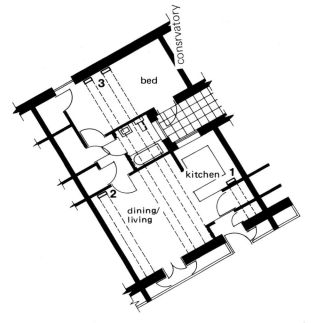

191 Plan

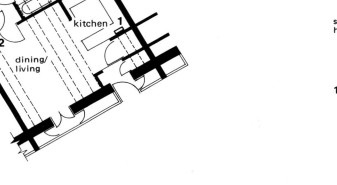

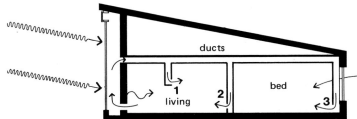

192 Winter operation

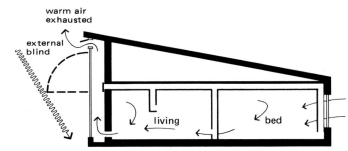

193 Summer operation

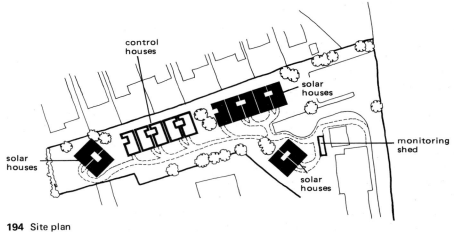

194 Site plan

195 View from west showing the five-terrace solar block

HUDDAKNOWL HOUSE

Address: The Edge, near Stroud, Gloucestershire
Architect: Angi and Alan Pinder
Solar engineer: John Willoughby
Date occupied: December 1978

The client acquired this site on the Cotswold escarpment, overlooking the Severn Vale, after World War II. By the early 1950's he had built a house on it. He then acquired an adjoining piece of land, and proposed to build a new house using stone salvaged from some existing cottages already on the site. He contacted the Landscape Institute in order to identify a local landscape architect who could prepare a landscape plan, locating the position of the house that would then be designed by a separately commissioned architect. In Gloucestershire consultants Angi and Alan Pinder, he found both landscape architect and architect. At an early design stage, the Pinders sought advice on energy conservation from John Willoughby, a fellow lecturer at the Cheltenham School of Art. His initial report suggested changes. The 170 m^2, two storey, three bedroom house should be orientated due south, and a conservatory added to protect the house from the south-westerly winds. Willoughby also suggested added insulation, controlled ventilation and solar heating.

ENERGY CONSERVATION

The external walls are insulated with 100 mm of glass fibre and 150 mm insulating concrete block inner leaf wall. They are faced with either Cotswold stone or horizontal boarding (U-values of 0.3 and 0.34 W/m^2°C respectively). The concrete ground floor consists of a 15 mm waterproof asphalt screed, a 100 mm slab and two layers of 50 mm glass fibre insulation (U-value of 0.27 W/m^2°C). The concrete tiled roof has 150 mm of insulation at ceiling level (U-value of 0.21 W/m^2°C). All windows are double glazed. A draught lobby is provided to the back door, and the front door is well protected. A mechanical ventilation system fitted with a heat recovery device cost about £1000 and will save about £75 annually. These measures reduce the peak heat loss rate to 4.1 kW and the annual space heating load to 7250 kWh. The heated plan area is 145 m^2.

PASSIVE HEATING

A solar greenhouse heated mode is employed. The 13.5 m^2 plan area of the attached conservatory has an effective collector area of 21 m^2. The timber framed glass roof is set at a pitch of 25°. Thermal storage is provided by a 16 m^3 rock store, located under the dining room floor, in the void created by the change in site levels. The rocks are single sized 100 mm diameter limestone. The rock store is insulated with 50 mm expanded polystyrene, and its floor is laid to a fall to facilitate drainage of any condensate. When air in the conservatory is hotter than the rock store, a 72 W fan extracts air via a 425 mm by 95 mm plywood duct. Air returns to the conservatory via a 130 mm diameter underflow metal duct that terminates in a floor grille. When heat

is required in the conservatory, air is extracted from the rock store via a second fan located at low level in the conservatory. The system is designed to provide heat only to the conservatory, dining and living room areas. Auxiliary heating is provided by a 13 kW oil fired boiler that distributes heat via Runtal radiators.

ACTIVE HEATING

A liquid flat plate collector system is used. An 11 m^2 array of panels can provide heat for the 40 m^3 swimming pool or the 245 litre combined solar/dhws cylinder. Over an average year this could contribute 5000 kWh of energy, providing a fuel saving of about £70.

PERFORMANCE

No monitoring has been undertaken to date, but provision has been made should funds become available.

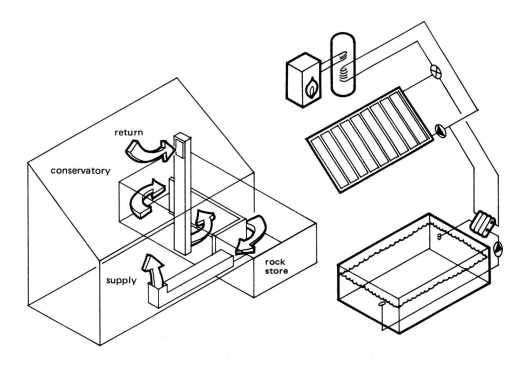

196 Solar system

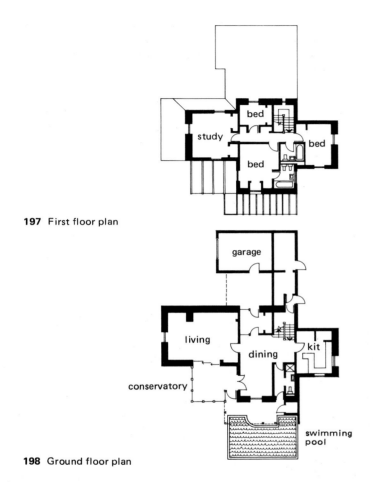

197 First floor plan

198 Ground floor plan

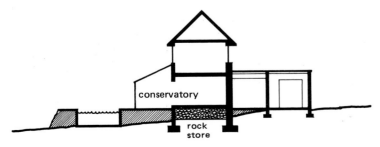

199 Section

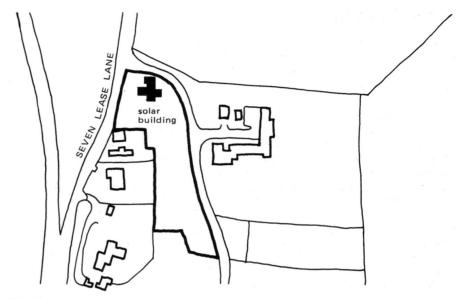

200 Site plan

201 View from south-west showing conservatory and solar collectors

Catalogue

DUDGEON HOUSE

Address:	Potton End, Hertfordshire
Architect:	Helix Multi Professional Services
Solar engineer:	Helix Multi Professional Services
Date occupied:	December 1978

The client requested a house that would be a low energy user. Any back up heating was to be provided as far as possible by alternative energy. The architect, Julian Keable, decided that an underfloor heating system would provide a flexible design solution, and that an attached conservatory running the full length of the house would enable the disabled client to enjoy a sunny environment without having to cope with the vagaries of the outdoors. The two storey, three bedroom, 166 m^2 house was completed in 1978 for about £25,000. It was constructed by a local builder working on a time basis, the services of the architect not being used in the construction stage.

ENERGY CONSERVATION
The brick/block external walls have a foam filled cavity (U-value of 0.60 W/m^2°C). The floor screed is insulated from the 150 mm concrete slab by a 40 mm polystyrene board, that has pre-formed recesses to carry the underfloor heating coils (U-value of 0.50 W/m^2°C). The pitched tiled roof is insulated with 150 mm glass fibre (U-value of 0.25 W/m^2°C). The windows are double glazed, and a draught lobby is provided. The peak heat loss rate is calculated at 6.2 kW, and the annual space heating load at 8000 kWh.

PASSIVE HEATING
A solar greenhouse heating mode is used. The conservatory attached to the south side of the house has a plan area of 24.3 m^2 and an effective collector area of 40 m^2. This represents 24% of the floor area. The patent glazing roof of the conservatory is pitched at 20° and nearby deciduous trees will impose some overshadowing. Thermal storage is provided by the concrete floor slab and brick walls. Internal greenhouse blinds provide protection from direct radiation, and overheated air can be vented to the ridge of the building by twelve ducts in the roof space that are controlled by plywood flaps located in the conservatory. Auxiliary heat for both space and water heating is provided by a 10.7 kW gas fired boiler as well as a solid fuel boiler. Domestic hot water is preheated by 2.68 m^2 of solar panel located just under the conservatory glass roof.

PERFORMANCE
The building is not being monitored. The large collector area would, however, suggest that solar heating will satisfy a substantial proportion of the space heating load.

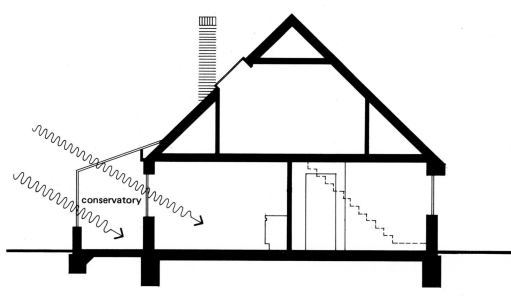

202 Section

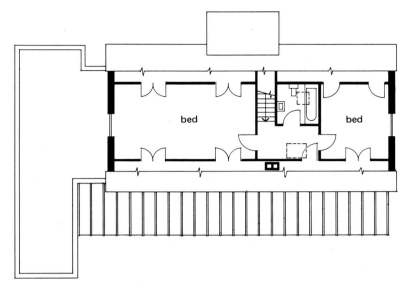

203 First floor plan

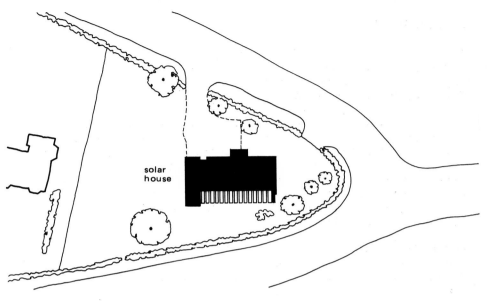

205 Site plan

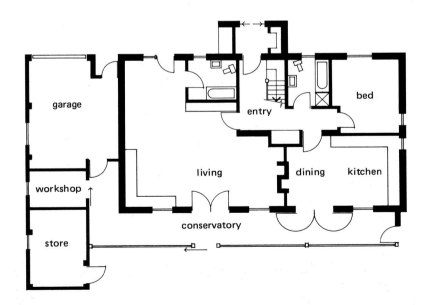

204 Ground floor plan

206 View from south-east showing full length conservatory

Catalogue

SALFORD HOUSES

Address: 4 and 6 Strawberry Hill, Wallness, Salford, Manchester, Lancashire
Architect: Salford City Technical Services Department (Architectural Division)
Solar engineer: Dr J.E. Randell, University of Salford
Date occupied: January 1979

Following the 1973 oil crisis, Salford City Council examined their housing policy to see if energy consumption could be reduced. In 1975 they approached the University of Salford with a view of jointly designing low energy housing. Preliminary technical discussions in 1976 established the design strategy of a highly insulated building shell heated by heat pumps, using warm but stale air extracted from the house as the heat source. Approval in principle for this was given in May 1977, and in June 1978, construction began on a prototype semi-detached pair of two storey, two bedroom houses. The Council stresses the experimental nature of these two houses that have now been completed at a cost of about £14,000 each, and await the results of monitoring before releasing a fully detailed account. They must, however, be pleased with preliminary measurements, since the second phase of the experiment is under construction on a site next door to the original houses. It is due for completion in March 1980.

ENERGY CONSERVATION

Generally, a 200 mm thick insulating overcoat was constructed around the thermally massive interior shell. Both skins of the brick/block exterior cavity walls were constructed as structurally independent. The exterior skin of the gable wall was strengthened with protruding, but not bridging, internal piers, while the internal skin is stiffened by the internal walls of the house. Wall ties occur only at three levels; the ground level, the first floor level and the roof level. The 173 mm wall cavity is filled with blown polyurethane granules. The ground floor is also insulated with poly-urethane granules (but a 200 mm thickness) blown in when the precast solid block/concrete beam floor system (also used on the first floor) was nearly finished. Around the perimeter of the ground floor, the underfloor insulation is turned down to the top of the footings in a 300 mm thickness. The 173 mm cavity wall insulation is also carried down to this level. The section of cavity wall below ground level was strengthened with headers at ground floor level to support the wall during backfilling. The foil-backed plasterboard ceiling is insulated with 200 mm of blown glass fibre. Standard window area (15 m^2) and orientation were retained, but the thermal efficiency was improved by using two sets of sliding windows set 50 mm apart in a common timber frame. The single glazed entrance door is protected from direct weather and the rear door opens onto a draught lobby. Humid and stale air is extracted continuously, but exclusively, from the kitchen, bathroom and toilet at the rate of three air changes per hour (ac/h) which corresponds to half an ac/h for the whole house. Uncontrolled leakage accounts for another half ac/h, making the total ventilation rate for the whole house one air change per hour. These measures have reduced the peak heat loss rate to 2.5 kW, and the specific heat loss rate to 100 W/^{o}C. The high thermal capacity is capable of making the best use of incidental heat gains, and continuous heating reduced the risk of condensation occurrence.

ACTIVE HEATING

A heat pump system is employed. It was chosen for three reasons. First, the cost of heat supplied was low at 0.423 p/kWh (assuming a COP of 2.5 and the use of Economy 7 night tariff at 1.508 p/kWh). Second, the heat pump could use different sources of low grade heat (e.g. solar heated water). Third, the system could easily integrate other sources of low grade heat (e.g. solar heated water).

The heat supply system is the same for each house. The source of heat is warm stale air extracted from the house. During the day it is blown over two wall mounted metal tanks that contain 85 litres of ice each. By continuously providing 700 W of heat, it melts the ice into water. For seven hours a night, the water is turned back into ice by two 325 W heat pumps. The extract heat is transferred to the heat distribution system, that differs for each house. A third 250 W heat pump is also used to extract heat directly from the extracted air.

House Type "A" (No 6) has a "dry" distribution system. For the seven hours at night, the heat pumps transfer heat from the ice tanks to a closed circuit of air. Twelve vertical stacks of bricks contained in a 450 mm wide cavity internal wall are warmed as the air circulates past them. These bricks provide thermal storage. Heat is further distributed by another closed air circuit to a void, created by having the plasterboard ceiling battened off the underside of the first floor slab. The occupants of the house are warmed by the large low temperature radiant panels of the first floor slab and the cavity walls of the brick filled internal wall.

House Type "B" (No 4) has a "wet" distribution system. For the seven hours at night, heat pumps transfer heat from the ice tanks to an underfloor heating system. The concrete floors act as the thermal mass. The underfloor coils consist of 180 m of 12.5 mm diameter reinforced PVC hosepipe fixed to the floor with neoprene bands and covered with a 75 mm screed. The coils are arranged in 30 m loops, taken off headers. Auxiliary heat is provided by a 3 kW immersion heater.

Both systems are controlled by a thermostat in the living room. Both systems have the heat pumps and ice tanks located in an external lean-to, for noise isolation. Domestic hot water for both systems is preheated from 10°C to 35/40°C by a fourth heat pump (100 W air/water) that also uses the warm stale extracted house air as the heat source. It transfers the heat to a 135 litre preheat cylinder connected in series to the 225 litre domestic hot water cylinder.

PERFORMANCE

Monitoring over the 1979/80 winter will be conducted by Dr Randell, but initial measurements indicate that the cost of space heating lies in the region predicted by theoretical analysis, approximately £30 per year. Water heating is expected to add another £40 per year to the fuel bill.

In the second phase of the experiment, the "dry" system has been abandoned and the four houses and two flats will use a modified "wet" system, consisting of a single 750 W water/water heat pump that provides background heating via underfloor coils. Individual room "topping up" will be provided by gas or electric off-peak room heaters. One of the heat pumps will be gas driven.

The predicted results appear hopeful and a full analysis at the end of the experiment is eagerly awaited.

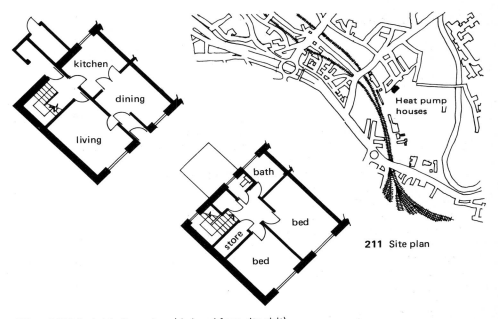

211 Site plan

209 and **210** Probable floor plans (deduced from site visit)

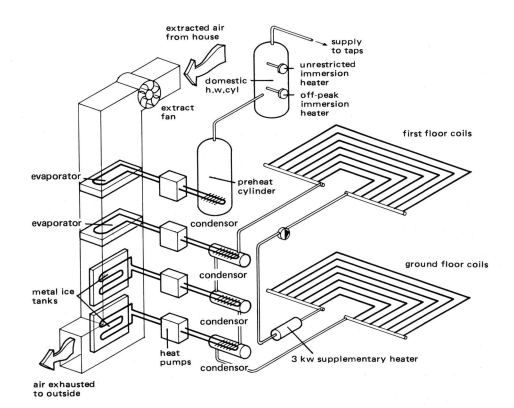

207 Heat pump arrangement

208 Heat distribution for "wet" system

212 View from north showing the lean-to containing the heat pump equipment

Catalogue

NORTHLANDS 1

Address :   Ashlyns Road, Basildon, Essex
Architect: Ahrends, Burton and Koralek (ABK)
Solar engineer :   ABK, George Kasabov, Ove Arup and Partners
Date occupied: January 1979 onwards

Ahrends, Burton and Koralek (ABK) first began working with the Basildon Development Corporation in the mid 1960's and had already done several housing schemes around the new town of Basildon. Work on the new suburb of Northlands was begun in 1974 with a combined study by ABK, Clive Plumb (who designed the Plumb House) and the Development Corporation. However, a lessening of the Corporation's work load in other areas meant that most of the design work for this project was done by the Corporation alone. But by the end of the year, ABK had been commissioned to fully develop one part of the suburb, Northlands 1. It was to contain 423 houses, both double and single storey and provide accommodation ranging from one to five bedrooms. Using the principles established by George Kasabov (who worked with ABK as a consultant in conjunction with Ove Arup and Partners) a scheme was developed that had energy conservation and passive solar heating as important design parameters. Kasabov's guidelines were established under seven headings: microclimate, site layout, environmental conditions, building shape, internal planning, construction and mechanical services.

ENERGY CONSERVATION

The site layout was considered first. Shelter belts of trees run north/south, with bands of housing in between. All houses were designed to face within 22° of south (to maximise solar gain) and careful spacing of the terraces (usually not less than 11 metres apart for double storey units) ensured that overshadowing was minimised. Terrace lengths were kept between 3 and 8 units. The ratio of building surface to volume was kept to a minimum and pitched roofs were incorporated to reduce wind turbulence as well as to provide ideal sites for future solar collectors. (In fact twelve such units (each 5.5 m^2) have now been installed).

The houses are energy consciously designed also. The brick cavity walls have 50 mm of cavity insulation (U-value of 0.5 W/m$^{2\circ}$C) and the timber boarded walls have 100 mm of insulation behind. The pitched tiled roofs have 75 mm of insulation at ceiling level (U-value of 0.54 W/m$^{2\circ}$C). Windows are single glazed and draught lobbies are provided. For a typical 88 m^2 two storey house, these measures reduce the peak heat loss rate to about 3.5 kW and the annual space heating load to 7500 kWh.

PASSIVE HEATING

Direct gain heating is employed. The major glazed areas of all houses face within 22° of south. The collector area, however, is low, generally only about 10 % of the floor area. Thermal storage is provided by the brick internal walls and concrete floor slabs. Insulating shutters were planned for movable insulation, but at the moment only curtains are installed. The main source of heating is provided by three coal fired boilers that distribute hot water to groups of houses (about 150 houses in a group). The water is carried by insulated overhead mains. Within the houses, heat is supplied by low pressure thermostatically controlled radiators, with costs allocated to individual tenants on a time basis.

PERFORMANCE

Monitoring is currently being carried out on ten of the houses by the Building Research Establishment. No results are yet available. It has been estimated though, by the designers, that direct gain heating will satisfy more than 10% of the space heating load. This percentage could be increased by improving the collector area/floor area ratio, provided that there is an improvement in the movable insulation. External overhangs or blinds may also reduce summer overheating.

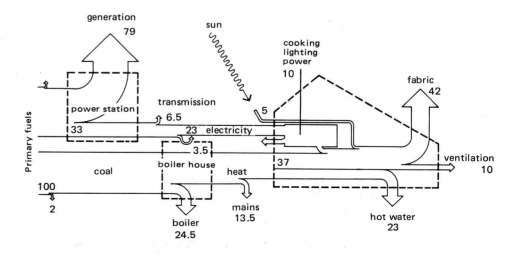

213 Annual energy use diagram

214 First floor plan for typical 5-person house

215 Ground floor plan for typical 5-person house

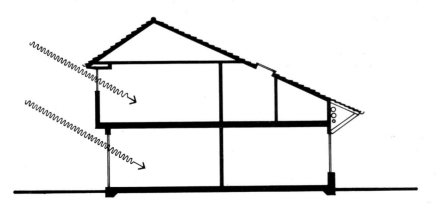

216 Section

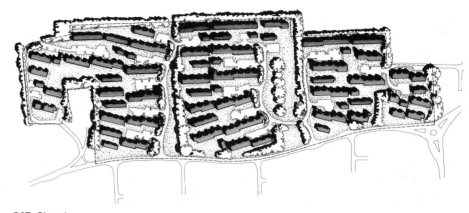

217 Site plan

218 General view showing pitched roof and south facing windows

Catalogue

THE HORSE AND GATE

Address: Witcham Toll, Sutton, near Ely, Cambridgeshire
Architect: Brenda and Robert Vale
Solar engineer: Brenda and Robert Vale
Date occupied: Attached conservatory occupied May 1979

The Horse and Gate was a pub probably built in about 1870. It is located at the intersection of two lonely roads that cut across the farmland forming the Isle of Ely, a clay ridge set about 20 metres above the surrounding fenland. The pub was bought in 1973 by Brenda and Robert Vale, as the logical conclusion to work they had previously been doing. In 1972/73 Brenda Vale and two other friends completed a final year thesis at Cambridge University Architecture Department on autonomous housing. Thames and Hudson, the publishers, became interested, but it was not until 1975 that the book **The Autonomous House: Design and Planning for Self-Sufficiency** was published. Meanwhile during 1972/73, both the Vales joined the Technical Research Division set up by Alexander Pike at the Cambridge University Department of Architecture. Other members included John Littler, Randall Thomas, James Thring and Jerry Smith. At the end of a year, the Vales decided to do something practical, so the Horse and Gate was purchased and converted into a house. Since the two storey, three bedroom, 115 m² building was already connected to mains water, electricity and drainage, it was decided not to produce a fully autonomous (ie self-sufficient) house, but rather, concentrate on reducing the energy consumption by the use of insulation and to then use a mixture of conventional and "renewable" energy sources to meet the reduced heating load.

ENERGY CONSERVATION

The existing 110 mm or 225 mm brick walls were internally insulated with 50 mm of glass fibre (with polythene sheet on both sides) and lined with plasterboard/polyurethane laminate (U-value of 0.42W/m²ºC). This decision to insulate internally was taken after due regard to the following factors: ease of fixing; quick thermal response; unchanged external appearance; cost; reduced internal plan area; interstitial condensation; and rain penetration. The existing concrete floor slab was waterproofed with a coat of bituminous latex emulsion then covered with a layer of 12.5 mm expanded polystyrene. Sheets of 19 mm tongued and grooved chipboard were glued together to form a continuous lining on top of the insulation (U-value of 0.76 W/m²ºC). The roof was insulated with 150 mm of glass fibre (U-value of 0.27 W/m²ºC). The existing windows in the north elevation were double glazed with do-it-yourself kits, while the remaining windows have been replaced with low cost double windows. A draught lobby is provided and all openings weatherstripped. These measures reduce the peak heat loss rate to 4.5 kW and the annual space heating load to 11,500 kWh.

PASSIVE HEATING

A solar greenhouse heating mode is employed. The 38.7 m² attached conservatory has an effective collector area of 57 m², which represents 50% of the floor area. The conservatory roof is made from patent glazing fixed at 600 mm centres, pitched at 25º and glazed with 4 mm horticultural glass. Thermal storage is provided by the brick walls, the concrete floor and water filled containers. A fish pond that is under construction will further add to the thermal storage. Shutters made of plywood and filled with polystyrene provide movable insulation to all openings between the house and the conservatory. Summer overheating is eliminated by opening vents at the ridge of the conservatory. Heat collected in the conservatory is distributed to the house by opening the doors and windows that interconnect. Auxiliary heating is provided by a 1 kW solid fuel Aga and a 7.9 kW wood burning stove. Domestic hot water is preheated by an 11 m² trickle type collector connected to a 180 litre preheat cylinder. It is located directly under the glass of the conservatory and forms the ceiling to the dining room projection.

PERFORMANCE

The Vales are monitoring the performance of the house using thermographs and a Stevenson screen. No results are available for a heating season that includes the contribution of the solar greenhouse, but the high collector area/floor area ratio should ensure a most significant contribution. The scheme might be improved by the use of an isolated, insulated rock store to conserve excess daytime heat for night time use within the thermally lightweight house. This is the first and only solar building at the moment that uses really effective movable insulation.

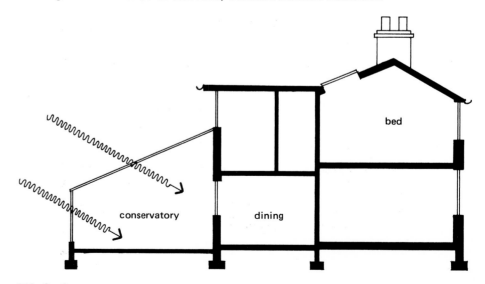

219 Section

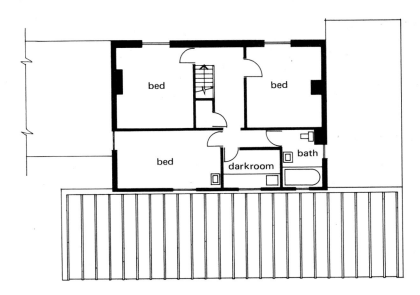

220 First floor plan

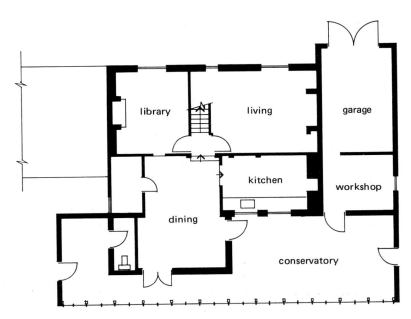

221 Ground floor plan

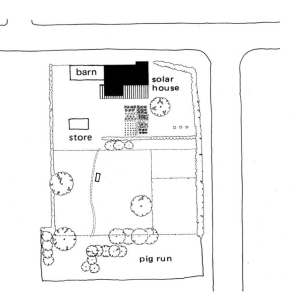

222 Site plan

223 View of full length conservatory with brick end wall

Catalogue

KIPPFORD HOUSE

Address: 16 Feu, Quarry Rd, Kippford, Kirkcudbrightshire, Scotland
Solar engineer: James R. Briggs and Associates
Date occupied: July 1979

After holidaying with her family in the surrounding area for several years, Mrs B. Hartshorne chanced across a fifth of a hectare of high land at Kippford that was for sale. It had a magnificent view as well as the partially completed structure of a building being erected to the previous owner's design. The land was purchased at the end of 1976 and Mrs. Hartshorne had the original design amended as far as possible to meet her own specific requirements. Unavoidable limitations, however, were imposed both by the existing structure as well as by the planning permission already granted by the local authority. What resulted was a 390 m^2 four bedroom, three storey holiday house, that would be intermittently occupied by the Hartshornes throughout the year. It was decided to incorporate a solar system to provide background heating in the winter months to prevent either condensation or frost damage occurring while the building was unoccupied. This meant that an internal air temperature of 8/10°C had to be maintained during these periods.

ENERGY CONSERVATION

The exterior walls have an outer leaf of brickwork, with a 32 mm cavity, then 25 mm of Jablite polystyrene boards that are fixed to the inner leaf of 150 mm breeze block (U-value of 0.6 W/m^2°C). All living area floors that are in direct contact with the ground are protected by 50 mm of insulating polystyrene board and the ceiling is insulated with 75 mm of mineral fibre quilt (U-value of 0.3 W/m^2°C). All windows are double glazed. The building has a calculated peak heat load of 21 kW.

ACTIVE HEATING

An air flat plate collector system is employed. It was chosen to eliminate the possibility of the heat transfer fluid freezing (as water could in a liquid flat plate collector system). The vertical collectors face 42° west of south with an effective area of 20 m^2; they are timber framed and traditionally glazed with 3 mm low iron content glass. The absorber plate consists of an aluminium sheet painted with Nextel (as at Milton Keynes) and pinned to the timber structure at the sides. The 50 mm gap between the glass and absorber plate is divided into two by a plane of staggered, horizontal 15 mm diameter copper pipes (in length a total of 1150 m) that provide solar heated water for the proposed 11 m by 4.3 m swimming pool. Insulated air ducts connect the solar air collectors to a room plenum fourteen metres away, and when the air in the collectors is approximately 5°C hotter than air in the room plenum, a fan circulates air from the collectors to the plenum and back again. This room plenum provides the supply air for the traditionally ducted warm air heating system.

If the air from the solar collectors is not sufficiently warm enough, a control closes off the collector and brings into operation two 12 kW electric storage heaters located in the room plenum. The solar system is also closed off when the swimming pool is in use, and solar heating is required.

A similarly constructed air flat plate collector array is also used to preheat water for the domestic hot water service.

PERFORMANCE

The partially predetermined layout and shape of the building has led to an unfortunate solar panel orientation (S42°W) and inclination (vertical) as well as necessitating a rather tortuous path for the solar air ducting systems. The construction of the air collectors may be suspect if high stagnation temperatures are reached (up to 150°C) and the small area of collector in relation to the heating load may result in an uneconomic break-even point. It will be interesting however to review the performance and cost-effectiveness of this site built system after several years of operation.

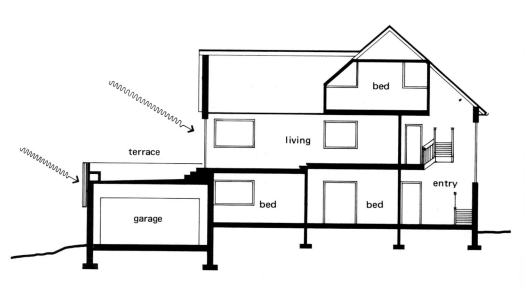

224 Section

225 Second floor plan

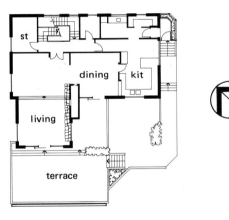

226 First floor plan

227 Ground floor plan

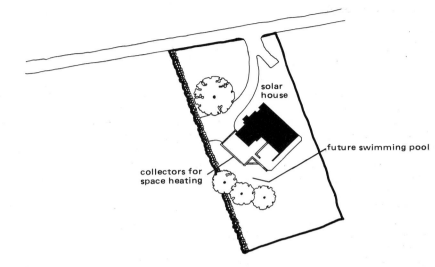

228 Site plan

229 View from south-east showing vertical collectors below terrace

Catalogue

REDFERN ROAD

Address: Redfern Road, off Brownhill Road, Catford, London SE6
Architect: Royston Summers
Solar Engineer: Max Fordham and Partners
Date occupied: Occupancy expected December 1979

Twenty-nine elderly peoples' flats are being constructed in a three storey block with the entire area of south facing roof to be occupied by 200 m^2 of liquid flat plate collector at a pitch of 51°. The collector tilt has been optimised for spring and autumn use and the system is expected to provide 40 per cent of the combined space heating and water load. Space heating is distributed to the ground floor flats only via 25 mm stainless steel pipes set into the 75 mm screed that rests on the 150 mm concrete slab. The whole system has been incorporated within the Parker Morris cost yard stick. It is anticipated that the system will be monitored.

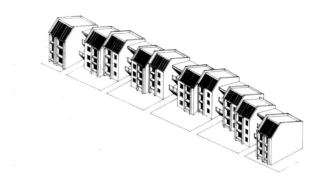

230   Redfern Road development

LINFORD 20A

Address: Great Linford, Buckinghamshire
Architect: Solar Energy Developments
Solar engineer: Solar Energy Developments
Date occupied: Occupancy expected December 1979

Nine 101 m^2, two storey, three bedroom fully detached family homes form the basis of an evaluation experiment jointly being undertaken by John Laing Research and Development Ltd and The Calor Group Ltd, with financial support being provided by the Department of Energy. Three of the houses have standard gas fired ducted warm air heating systems and act as the control houses; a further three houses have 18 m^2 of liquid flat plate collector incorporated into a solar assisted heat pump system developed by John Laing R & D: and the last three houses include 40 m^2 of collector linked to a system being developed by Calor. All collectors are inclined at 45° and face due south. All nine houses will be extensively monitored.

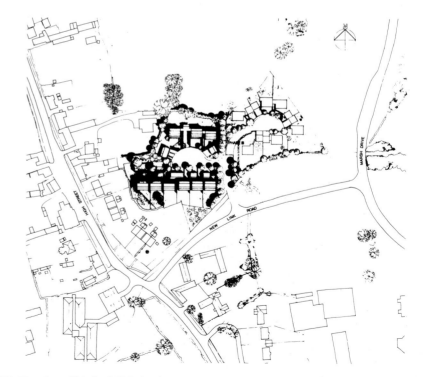

231   Site plan of Linford 20A development

232 Perspective of Miller Homes development

MILLER HOMES

Address: Buckstone, near Edinburgh
Architect: Miller Homes Northern Limited
Solar Engineer: Calor Group Ltd , Fulmer Research Institute, Solar Energy
                   Developments
Date occupied: Occupancy expected December 1979

At their 600 home housing estate at Buckstone, Miller Homes are erecting a solar house that uses a solar heating and storage system patented by Calor. It consists of 28 m^2 of copper collector linked to a heat storage unit containing 560 kilograms of chemical phase change material. This chemical heat store is small enough to fit into a cupboard. An energy saving of fifty per cent is predicted with the system, and monitoring will be conducted by Napier College over the next two winters. The project is a continuation of Calor's development programme that was being carried out with the Fulmer Research Institute and Solar Energy Developments.

NEWINGTON GREEN ROAD

Address: 79-81 Newington Green Road, Islington, London N1
Architect: Robert Fawcett
Solar engineer: Robert Fawcett in conjunction with Edward Curtis
Date occupied: Occupancy expected January 1980

Eleven two-person flats are being constructed in a four storey block on a small site bounded on the east by a busy road and the south by a railway line. The flats are well insulated: cavity foam wall insulation; 150 mm glass fibre roof insulation; 25 mm urethane foam insulation to the underside of screeds; and double glazing used for both sound and thermal insulation. A passive thermal storage wall is employed in three flats. The unvented Trombe wall consists of a concrete filled cavity brick wall, painted black and glazed on the outside. Inside, a 75 mm false plasterboard stud wall is set 100 mm clear of the masonry wall, with hit-and-miss ventilators controlling the flow of heated air. These collectors are vertical, situated beneath the living room and bedroom windows and face approximately south-west. The system will be monitored by the Polytechnic of North London.

233 Site plan of Newington Green Road development

Catalogue

LINFORD 8B

Address: Great Linford, Buckinghamshire
Architect: The Charter Building Design Group
Solar Engineer: Milton Keynes Development Corporation, Energy Consultative Unit
                  in conjunction with the Open University Energy Research Group
Date occupied: Occupancy expected May 1980

A private developer, S and S Homes Ltd, in conjunction with the Private Housing Unit of the Milton Keynes Development Corporation, is erecting eight direct gain passive solar homes in their eighty-eight house development at Great Linford. The two storey, four bedroom, 110 m² houses are for private sale and are similar in construction to the very highly insulated Pennyland homes. Extensive monitoring will be carried out for three years by the Energy Research Group at the Open University, with funding provided by the Energy Technology Support Unit.

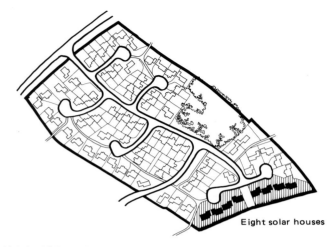

Eight solar houses

234 Site plan of Linford 8B development

PENNYLAND

Address: Pennyland, Milton Keynes
Architect: Milton Keynes Development Corporation Architects
Solar engineer: Milton Keynes Development Corporation, Energy Consultative Unit
                  in conjunction with the Open University, Energy Research Group
Date occupied: Occupancy expected July 1980

The Pennyland One site comprises 177 local authority houses that are divided into two groups; the first consisting of 94 highly insulated houses and the second of 83 very highly insulated houses. They are all two storey, range from one to five bedrooms and are built to Parker Morris standards. The very highly insulated houses have 100 mm cavity fill external walls with fibre fill, 150 mm loft insulation, 25 mm perimeter slab insulation, with all windows being double glazed and fitted with insulating shutters or blinds. A typical peak heat loss rate for an end terrace house is 160 W/$^{\circ}$C compared to a traditionally built house of 315 W/$^{\circ}$C. Direct gain passive solar heating has been maximised by ensuring correct orientation (most buildings face due south and all buildings face within 45° of south) and using large areas of south facing glass coupled with movable insulation shutters. Gas fired boilers linked to thermostatically controlled radiators provide the auxiliary back up. Extensive monitoring of 60 houses on this site will be used to compare the performance of 20 traditionally built houses on another site.

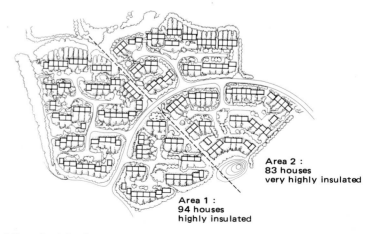

Area 2 :
83 houses
very highly insulated

Area 1 :
94 houses
highly insulated

235 Site plan of Pennyland development

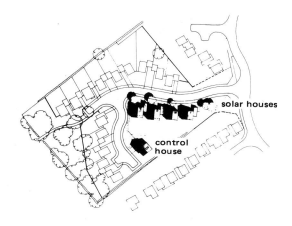

236 Site plan of Foxhills development

FOXHILLS

Address: Two Furlong Lane, Foxhills, Aylesbury
Architect: Solar Energy Developments
Solar engineer: Solar Energy Developments
Date occupied: Occupancy expected summer 1980

Taylor Woodrow Homes Ltd are erecting four passive solar houses at their Foxhills Estate, Aylesbury. Each house design is based on a standard Taylor Woodrow four bedroom, detached, two storey house type, modified to provide four different passive solar heating modes: direct gain; solar greenhouse; Trombe wall; and water wall. These 109 m^2 solar homes are designed so that approximately half of their space heating load is satisfied by the solar systems. Domestic hot water will also be solar preheated. The performance of the solar houses will be evaluated against the performance of a control house for a period of four years: the first year unoccupied, the next three years occupied. The monitoring will be conducted by Taylor Woodrow Research Laboratories.

SHAVINGTON

Address: Rope Lane, Shavington, near Crewe, Cheshire
Architect: Cheshire County Council Department of Architecture
Solar engineer: Cheshire County Council Department of Architecture and the Shell
                  Research Centre, Thornton
Date occupied: Occupancy expected August 1980

This forty place, 1200 m^2, two storey elderly persons' home follows on from the Sandbach County Primary School, and represents the next step in the Cheshire County Council's energy conservation programme. The liquid flat plate system consists of 200 m^2 of collector at a $22\frac{1}{2}^{\circ}$ pitch, integrated into the south facing part of the roof. The collectors are linked to three thermal water storage tanks (18000, 4500 and 900 litres) with the heat distributed by thermostatically controlled high efficiency convector radiators. Auxiliary heat is provided by three oil fired boilers. A monitoring programme will be conducted by the Council and the Shell Research Centre, with funds made available from the Department of Energy.

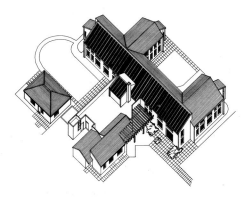

237 Shavington development

Catalogue

WALTON "THE GUNFLEET" (TENDRING HIGH) SCHOOL

Address: Rochford Way, Frinton-on-Sea, Essex
Architect: Essex County Architect's Department
Solar engineer: Essex County Architect's Department
Date occupied: Occupancy expected September 1980

When asked to provide an additional 120 places in 1000 m^2 of teaching accommodation for humanities and business studies at an existing comprehensive school, the Essex County Architect's Department developed the approach already established at the Roach Vale C.P. School. The deep plan and M.C.B. construction technique was employed, but the central courtyard was greatly enlarged and covered in a standard greenhouse at roof level to create a solarium below that supplies solar heated air as the heat source to two air/water heat pumps (each 35 kW output). Heated water from the heat pumps is piped to ceiling mounted fan convectors that warm supply air, with stale air being extracted into the solarium for maximum heat extraction via the heat pumps, before being finally exhausted to atmosphere.

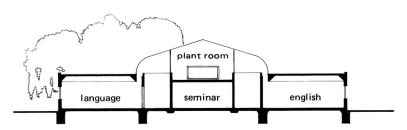

238 Section through Walton "The Gunfleet" (Tendring High) School development

THE SHED

Address: Sunbury Court, Westbourne Road, Sheffield 10
Architect: Ecotecture Group
Solar engineer: Ecotecture Group
Date occupied: Occupancy of the complete building expected by September 1980

Further to the building of Delta, Cedric Green has developed his ideas, and now heads (amongst other University activities) the Ecotecture Group in the Architecture Department at Sheffield University. This group is now building an experimental, timber framed, single storey, low energy solar building, that is designed to improve on the thermal performance experienced by Delta. The Shed scheme employs the same passive solar greenhouse heating mode, but the collector/floor area ratio has been increased from 1:3 to 1:1, and three different thermal storage systems are to be evaluated. Stage 1 (approximately half the area of the finished house) was complete in October 1978 and some preliminary thermal measurements begun. On completion, the project will be fully monitored by the Ecotecture Group.

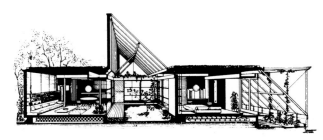

239 Section through The Shed showing complete development

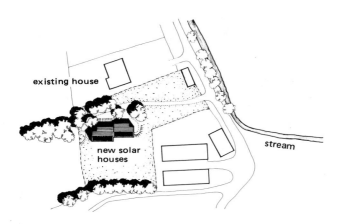

240 Site plan of Bore Place farmhouses

BORE PLACE FARMHOUSES

Address: Chiddingstone, Edenbridge, Kent
Architect: Helix multi professional services
Solar engineer: Helix multi professional services
Date occupied: Occupancy expected late 1980

Having recently completed a methane digestor scheme at Neil Wates' farm in Kent that provided power from the manure produced by the milking herd, Helix were next asked to provide additional living accommodation in the form of two farmhouses, each to be three bedroom. Helix proposed, and were enthusiastically backed by the client, a passive solar greenhouse scheme for the two storey 93 m^2 houses. The ground floor has a full length conservatory and the first floor a full length air flat plate collector. The combined collector area is fifty-two per cent on the floor area and is expected to satisfy 80 per cent of the 2000 kWh space heating load. The designers are hopeful that the scheme will be monitored.

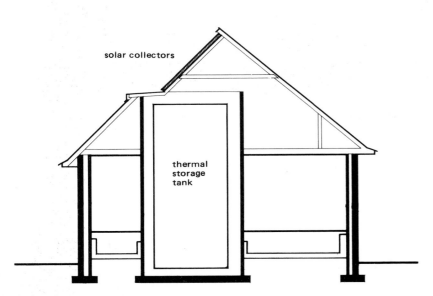

241 Section through Cunningham house

CUNNINGHAM HOUSE

Address: Townend Terrace, Kilmarnock, Ayrshire
Designer: Robert Cunningham, M.Sc.
Solar engineer: Robert Cunningham, M.Sc.
Date occupied: Occupancy expected December 1980

Robert Cunningham has designed and is now building his own solar home in Scotland. The 100 m^2, single storey, three bedroom home is well insulated: 100 to 150 mm of cavity wall insulation; 200 mm of glass fibre ceiling insulation, and underfloor insulation. A heat recovery ventilation system is also provided. Cunningham calculates the peak heat loss at 235 W/$^{\circ}$C, and the annual space heating load at 15,500 kWh. A liquid flat plate collector solar heating system is employed; 45 m^2 of collector at a pitch of 45° is connected to a 22000 litre cylindrical steel water thermal storage tank. Heat is distributed via a ducted warm air system that incorporates a novel hollow concrete floor system. Auxiliary heating for the system is provided by electric immersion heaters in the water storage tank.

Catalogue

BIBLIOGRAPHY USED FOR THIS CHAPTER

CURTIS HOUSE

1   CURTIS, E.J.W. 'Solar Energy Applications in Architecture', *MARU,* The Polytechnic of North London, 2/74.

WALLASEY SCHOOL

2   MORGAN, E.A. 'Improvements in Solar Heated Buildings', *Patent Specification 1 022 411,* The Patent Office, London, 1966.
3   HITCHIN, E.R., THOMPSON, K., and WILSON, C.B. 'The thermal design and performance of St George's School, Wallasey', *Journal of the Institution of Heating and Ventilating Engineers,* pp 325-331, Vol 33, 1966.
4   LOVE, J.B. 'Economic comparison of the solar and conventionally heated sections of St George's Secondary Modern School, Wallasey', *TRG Report 1636, United Kingdom Atomic Energy Authority,* H.M.S.O., London, 1968.
5   MANNING, P. 'St George's School, Wallasey : an evaluation of a solar heated building', *Architects' Journal Information Library,* pp 1715-1721, 25 June 1969.
6   A REPORT TO THE NATIONAL RESEARCH DEVELOPMENT CORPORATION ON MR E.A. MORGAN'S TECHNIQUES OF BUILDING CONSTRUCTION FOR HEATING AND LIGHTING OF BUILDINGS.
7   DAVIES, M.G. 'The Contribution of Solar Gain to Space Heating', *Solar Energy,* Vol 18, pp 361-367, 1976.
8   DAVIES, M.G. Private communication.

MILTON KEYNES

9   HODGES, D. and HORTON, A. 'Milton Keynes Solar House : performance of solar heating system April 1975-March 1977 including cost analysis', Polytechnic of Central London, Built Environment Research Group.
10   STEPHEN GEORGE & PARTNERS. *European Solar Houses.* Update of Working Paper submitted to the Commission of the European Communities, September 1978.

ANGLESEY HOUSE

11   WRIGHT, J.B. 'The Anglesey Solar Bungalow — energy costs', *Sun at Work in Britain,* pp 11-17, No 4, December 1976.
12   WRIGHT, J.B. 'The Anglesey Solar Bungalow — energy costs, Part II', *Sun at Work in Britain,* pp 40-41, No 6, January 1978.

MACCLESFIELD HOUSE

13   WILSON, D.R. 'Solar collection and storage techniques in a house conversion at Macclesfield for Granada TV', *Proceedings,* Technical Meeting of UK-ISES, 20 October 1977.
14   MCLAUGHLIN, T.P. *'A House for the Future',* Independent Television Books Ltd, 1976.
15   STEPHEN, F.R. *'Performance Monitoring of Low Energy House, Macclesfield',* Electricity Council Research Centre Report ECRC/M1281, September 1979.

BLYTH HOUSE

16   WARD, I.C. 'An estimation of the performance of the solar heating system installed in a private house at Blyth, Notts', Department of Building Science, Faculty of Architectural Studies, University of Sheffield; publication BS37, December 1977.

WILSON HOUSE

17   NEAL, W.E.J. 'A solar assisted heat pump and storage system for domestic space and water heating using a conventional roof as a radiation absorber'. *Proceedings,* 1979 Silver Jubilee International Congress of the International Solar Energy Society, May 28-June 1 1979.

SANDBACH COUNTY PRIMARY SCHOOL

18   TANNER, T.W. 'Solar space and water heating at a Cheshire School', *Proceedings,* Practical Applications of Solar Energy in Industry and Commerce, International Solar Energy Society, Conference M1, September 1979.

ROACH VALE COUNTY PRIMARY SCHOOL

19   CROWE, R.W. and PAGE, P.A. *'Integrated Environmental Design of Schools',* Essex County Architect's Department.

HIGHER BEBINGTON

20   GREENWOOD, P. and WARD, H. 'Solar Houses for the Elderly, Acorn Close, Wirral', *Proceedings,* Conference (C19) The Passive Collection of Solar Energy in Buildings, International Solar Energy Society, UK Branch, April 1979.

THE HORSE AND GATE

21   VALE, R. 'Low cost thermal upgrading of an existing house', Report for Alternative Technology Group, Open University.

APPENDICES

- **Bibliography**
- **Organisations**
- **Architects and Solar Engineers**
- **Fuel Price Increases**
- **Fuel Equivalents**
- **Energy Consumption Rates**
- **Temperatures**
- **Heat Capacities**
- **S.I. Unit Prefixes**
- **Conversion Factors**

Appendices

APPENDIX A

BIBLIOGRAPHY

The list below represents an excellent cross section of the many books available, and for approximately £100 it is possible to obtain a most worthwhile and informative solar library.

OVERVIEWS

DIRECT USE OF THE SUN'S ENERGY
Farrington Daniels
Ballantine Paperbacks, New York, 1964, £1.00

Simple readable overview covering the entire field of harnessing the sun's energy.

SUNSPOTS
Steve Baer
Zomewards Corporation, Albrquerque, 1975

Freewheeling, freethinking kaleidoscope of ideas from this ingenious New Mexican scientist/builder, who firmly believes in the rights of the individual.

SUN POWER
J.C. McVeigh
Pergamon Press Ltd., Oxford, 1977. £2.75

A sober update to Daniel's book that concentrates on applying technology.

SOLAR ENERGY FOR MAN
B.J. Brinkworth
The Compton Press, Salisbury, 1972. £4.75

A more technical exposition from the leader of the Solar Energy Unit at University College, Cardiff.

APPROACHES

SMALL IS BEAUTIFUL
E.F. Schumacher
Abacus, London. £1.75

A positive way forward that respects the person rather than the product. Schumacher was the founder and director (till his death in 1977) of the London based firm, Intermediate Technology Developments Group Ltd.

THE ENERGY QUESTION
Gerald Foley
Pelican Books, London, 1976. £1.25

An excellent book that reviews the world's energy resources and consumption rates, and suggests that the time-span responsibility adopted in private lives becomes the normal standard for public and commercial affairs.

A LOW ENERGY STRATEGY FOR THE UNITED KINGDOM
Gerald Leach
Science Reviews, 1979. £7.50

This cool-headed look at the total question of energy consumption makes sober reading and offers a direct challenge to the energy policy makers and consumers of this country.

THE ARCHITECTURE OF THE WELL-TEMPERED ENVIRONMENT
Reyner Banham
Architectural Press, London 1969. £3.75

A classical text that assesses the impact of environmental engineering on the design of building and on the mind of architects during the past hundred years.

CLIMATE

DESIGN WITH CLIMATE
Victor Olgyay
Princeton University Press, Princeton, 1963. £19.10

A classical text that identifies optimum plan shapes and orientations, locates insulation and thermal mass in relation to climatic zones, then puts it all together in four house types.

MANUAL OF TROPICAL HOUSING AND BUILDING: PART I CLIMATIC DESIGN
Koenigsberger et al.
Longman Group Limited, New York, 1973. £4.70

A first-rate, very readable text that explains the basics of climatic design, be it London or Marrakesh.

HISTORICAL REVIEW

SOLAR HEATED BUILDINGS OF NORTH AMERICA
William A. Shurcliff
Brick House Publishing Co., New Hampshire, 1978.

A selected review of one hundred and twenty solar heated houses, classified state by state. Description by word, photograph and line drawing, sadly omitting plans. Nevertheless, essential early reading.

THE CLIMATE CONTROLLED HOUSE
House Beautiful
Series of monthly articles from October 1949 to January 1951.

Architects from all over America were selected to design a house appropriate to the climate of that state. These articles record those efforts.

THE GLASS HOUSE
John Hix
The MIT Press, Cambridge, Massachusetts, 1974.
Available from the London Art Bookshop. £15.35

This beautifully illustrated book traces the history of glass structures from their early beginnings to the present day, that makes both fascinating and relevant reading to the solar enthusiast.

GENERAL SOLAR DESIGN

THE SOLAR HOME BOOK
Bruce Anderson
Prism Press, 1976, £5.50.

Anderson's excellent grasp of the subject is evident in the easily understandable text and drawings. His material covers both space heating and space cooling, and shows how these systems can be integrated into buildings in the various American climates.

SOLAR ENERGY AND BUILDING
S.V. Szokolay
Architectural Press, London, 1975. £7.50

A primer for fledgling solar engineers who want to get a handle on the subject, as well as an extremely handy reference for building designers. Most components and systems are described and quantified, and a world wide review of solar buildings is included.

SOLAR HEATING, Sunset Homeowner guide to
Sunset Books
Lane Publishing Co., California, 1978

An extremely competent, complete and readable account from this reputable American publishing house. Beautifully illustrated, it represents the best summary for the solar "lay" person that I know. Once again it is directed specifically at the American market and American climate.

SPECIALIST SOLAR DESIGN

KEEPING WARM FOR HALF THE COST
Colesby and Townsend
Prism Press, 1976. £1.50

A clear simple guide to domestic energy conservation by the use of insulation.

NATURAL SOLAR ARCHITECTURE: A PASSIVE PRIMER
David Wright
Van Nostrand Reinhold Co., New York, 1978.

Exactly what the title says; a passive primer. Though the presentation is not to my taste, what Wright has to say is first-rate, as one would expect from one of the leading solar architects in California.

Appendices

DOMESTIC HEAT PUMPS
John A. Sumner
Prism Press, 1976. £2.95

This book, with its simpler companion, "Introduction to Heat Pumps", is probably the most readable text on this most underrated, if somewhat tricky, subject. Sumner is in his early 80s, and his Nottingham University teacher knew Lord Kelvin, the father of the heat pump.

SOLAR GREENHOUSE
Rick Fisher and Bill Yanda
John Muir Publications, Santa Fe, 1976. £4.00

This is THE textbook for the attached greenhouse, written in clear simple language by two people who build these structures all over America.

PRACTICAL SOLAR HEATING
Kevin McCartney
Prism Press, 1978. £2.50

An excellent guide to solar assisted domestic hot water installations. Aimed primarily at the do-it-yourself enthusiast, it is equally applicable to the designer, for it is written by a man who has much experience in the application of technology.

GOING SOLAR
J.C. McVeigh and D.C. Schumacher
Natural Energy Association, London, 1976. £0.95

This practical guide to domestic solar water heating is directed at the consumer, and by a question and answer technique explains the basic principles involved and gives guide lines in choosing a system.

TECHNICAL APPROACH

SOLAR ENERGY THERMAL PROCESSES
John A. Duffie and William A. Beckman
John Wiley and Sons, Inc. New York, 1974. £12.50

A quantitative approach to a whole range of thermal processes. More for the solar engineer than the solar architect, it is, however, an excellent reference by two of the acknowledged leaders in the American solar field.

APPLICATIONS OF SOLAR ENERGY FOR HEATING AND COOLING OF BUILDINGS
Edited by Richard C. Jordan and Benjamin Y.H. Liu
A.S.H.R.A.E. Inc., New York, 1977.

A collection of papers covering system components and performance, and their application in heating and cooling spaces. The papers have been written by a solar-studded array of authors.

MAGAZINES

SINGLE ISSUE REVIEWS
Bauen + Wohnen, July — August 1977
L'Architecture d'Aujourd'hui, September 1977
RIBA Journal, June 1978

CONTINUING INFORMATION SOURCES

SOUTHWEST BULLETIN
A monthly magazine available from:
New Mexico Solar Energy Association,
P.O. Box 2004, Santa Fe,
New Mexico 87501, U.S.A.

Membership $US 10 per annum

SUNWORLD (Quarterly)
SOLAR ENERGY (Bi-monthly)
A magazine and journal available by joining:

U.K. International Solar Energy Society,
19 Albemarle Street,
London W1X 3HA

Membership £20.00 per annum.

ARCHITECTURAL DESIGN
A monthly magazine that has occasional articles concerning solar energy. Available from:

42 Leinster Gardens
London W2

Annual Subscription £22.50

BUILDING RESEARCH ESTABLISHMENT (BRE) CURRENT PAPER
A continuing series of reports on research carried out at the Centre, available from:

Distribution Unit
Application Services Division
Building Research Establishment
Garston Watford WD2 7JR
England

Charges will be made for quantity, but generally the service is free.

SOLAR AGE
An excellent monthly magazine pitched at the interested lay person and written by American leaders in the field. Available from:

Solar Age
P.O. Box 4934
Manchester N.H. 03108
United States of America

Annual Subscription $US 26.

HELIOS
A quarterly newsletter devoted to solar energy utilization and related topics. Available from:

Solar Energy Unit
Department of Mechanical Engineering and Energy Studies
University College
Newport Road
Cardiff CF2 1TA

There is normally no charge since the publication is funded by the Department of Industry.

UNITED KINGDOM ORGANISATIONS

SOLAR TRADE ASSOCIATION LIMITED

The Building Centre
26 Store Street
London WC1E 7BT

Phone (01) 636 4717

An association of members of the solar trade who abide by a Code of Conduct. The Association can deal with complaints as well as provide information on installers, suppliers, etc.

PILKINGTON — SOLAR ENERGY ADVISORY SERVICE

Pilkington Bros. Ltd.
Prescot Road
St Helens Merseyside WA10 3TT

Phone (0744) 28882

Pilkingtons have been active in the solar energy field for some time and have been directly involved in several projects. Their advice then is based on sound reasoning and experience.

THE COPPER DEVELOPMENT ASSOCIATION

Orchard House
Mutton Lane
Potters Bar
Herts EN6 3AP

Phone (77) 50711

They provide a set of information sheets (that include several solar installations) as well as advising on the integration of copper into solar systems.

Appendices

NATIONAL CENTRE FOR ALTERNATIVE TECHNOLOGY

Llwyngwern Quarry
(3 miles north of Machynlleth on A487)
Machynlleth Powys Wales

Phone (0654) 2400

The centre is mainly a demonstration project to show that people can live happily on limited material resources without returning to the hardships of the past. It is well worth a visit. Books and information sheets are also available.

UK-ISES

19 Albemarle Street
London W1X 3HA

Phone (01) 493 6601

The U.K. section (founded in 1973) of the world wide International Solar Energy Society, itself founded in 1954 to act as a forum and centre for the exchange of information, as well as to stimulate interest in the possibilities of this inexhaustible source of energy. Membership is open to everyone. The U.K. section has many excellent publications for sale, and holds numerous conferences and meetings.

Annual subscription £20 for individuals

CHARTERED INSTITUTION OF BUILDING SERVICES (CIBS)

formerly the
INSTITUTION OF HEATING AND VENTILATING ENGINEERS (IHVE)

49 Cadogan Square
London SW1X 0JB

Phone (01) 235 7671

The Institution provides a remarkable set of guides covering design data, installation and equipment data and reference data, all of which are well worth having as a reference source.

SOLAR ENERGY UNIT

Department of Mechanical Engineering and Energy Studies
University College
Newport Road
Cardiff CF2 1TA

Phone (0222) 44211 ext 7116
Contact Dr C.M.A. Johansson, Information Officer

The Solar Energy Unit, set up by Professor B.J. Brinkworth in the mid-sixties, has accumulated a large body of knowledge and experience that it openly disseminates. Queries should be addressed to the Information Officer.

BUILDING SERVICES RESEARCH AND INFORMATION ASSOCIATION (BSRIA)

Old Bracknell Lane
Bracknell
Berkshire RG12 4AH

Phone (0344) 25071/5

On joining BSRIA a range of useful publications become available: application guides, project reports, technical notes, bibliographies, abstracts and statistics. Advice can also be given and monitoring equipment hired.

BUILDING RESEARCH ADVISORY SERVICE

Building Research Establishment
Garston
Watford WD2 7JR

Phone (09273) 74040

The advisory service handles queries from the general public. No charge is made for information available "off the shelf", but more detailed enquiries will have to be paid for on a consulting basis.

BUILDING REGULATIONS PROFESSIONAL DIVISION

Department of the Environment
Becket House
1 Lambeth Palace Road
London SE1 7ER

Phone (01) 211 8047

The division can advise on possible problem areas related to the UK building regulations and solar energy applications.

RADIATION SECTION – METEOROLOGICAL OFFICE

Headquarters Annexe
Bracknell
Berkshire RG12 2UR

Phone (0344) 20242 ext 2541

This Office is the source of insolation data throughout the U.K. A nominal charge (around £5) is made for straightforward enquiries, but more detailed information attracts higher charges (around £30). Weather tapes are also available.

EUROPEAN ORGANISATIONS

BELGIAN SECTION of ISES

Universite Libre de Bruxelles
Faculte des Sciences
Avenue F. D. Roosevelt 50
Bruxelles, Belgium

ITALIAN SECTION of ISES

Via Crispi 72
80121 Naples, Italy

SCANDINAVIAN SECTION of ISES

VVS-Tekniska Föreningen
Hantverkargatan 8
S-112 21 Stockholm, Sweden

FRANCE

Cooperation Mediterraneene Pour
L'energie Solaire (COMPLES)
Agence de la Rose
6, Route de la Croix-Rouge
13013, Marseilles, France

SWITZERLAND

Solar Energy Society of Switzerland
Eth Leonhardstr 27
CH-8001 Zurich
Switzerland

IRISH SECTION of ISES

School of Architecture, University College
Earlsfort Terrace
Dublin 2, Ireland

NETHERLANDS SECTION of ISES

Netherlands Energy Research Foundation
P.O. Box 1, 1755 ZG Petten
Holland

WEST GERMAN SECTION of ISES

VDI-Gesellschaft Energietechnik
4 Dusseldorf 1, Postfach 1139
Federal Republic of Germany

Appendices

ARCHITECTS AND SOLAR ENGINEERS

Below is a list of some of the consultants who have been involved in British solar projects in the past. They can be contacted for assistance on particular projects, but they should not be approached with general inquiries or requests for free information. General inquiries should be addressed to UK-ISES or the Solar Trade Association (see Appendix B). This list is by no means complete nor does it in any way constitute a warranty of the services of the firms listed.

ARCHITECTS

Ahrends Burton and Koralek
1 Spencer Court
Chalcot Road
London NW1
(01) 586 3311   Contact: Mr R. Burton

Peter Bond Partnership
The Dome
The Quadrant
Richmond
(01) 940 7491   Contact: Mr P. Bond

Robert Fawcett
National Westminster Chambers
Salisbury Square
Hatfield Hertfordshire AL9 5AF
(30) 61600

Helix Multi Professional Services
Mortimer Hill
Mortimer
Reading, Berkshire RG7 3PG
(0734) 333070   Contact: Mr J. Keable

Rod James
National Centre for Alternative Technology
Llwyngwern Quarry
Machynlleth
Wales
(0654) 2400

Angi and Alan Pinder
End Cottage
Guiting Power
Gloucestershire
(045 15) 546

Dominic Michaelis Associates
Bay 8
16 South Wharf Road
London W2 1PF
(01) 402 3203   Contact: Mr D. Michaelis

Royston Summers
3 North Several
London SE3 0QR
(01) 852 5346

Brenda and Robert Vale
The Horse and Gate
Witcham Toll
Sutton, near Ely
Cambridgeshire
(035 377) 8723

Donald Wilson
The Malt Kiln Studio Workshop
North Street
Owston Ferry
Humberside

SOLAR ENGINEERS

Ambient Energy Design
36 Apthorpe Street
Fulbourn
Cambridge CB1 5EY
(0223) 880518
Contact: Mr J. Littler

Ove Arup Partnership
13 Fitzroy Street
London W1
(01) 636 1531
Contact: Mr J. Campbell

Peter Bond Partnership
The Dome
The Quadrant
Richmond
(01) 940 7491
Contact: Mr P. Bond

James R. Briggs and Associates
Burdetts Mews
Belsize Crescent
Hampstead
London NW3 5QX
(01) 794 8233—7
Contact: Mr J. Briggs

Energy Conscious Design
5 Dryden Street
London WC1
(01) 240 2430
Contact: Mr D. Turrant

Energy Consultative Unit
Milton Keynes Development Corporation
Wavendon Tower
Wavendon
Milton Keynes MK17 8LX
(0908) 74000
Contact: Mr J. Doggart

Oscar Faber and Partners
18 Upper Marlborough Road
St Albans
(56) 59111
Contact: Mr P. Martin

Max Fordham and Partners
51b James Town Road
London NW1
(01) 267 5761
Contact: Dr N. Ryding

General Technology Systems
Forge House
20 Market Place
Brentford
(01) 568 5871
Contact: Mr B. McNelis

Helix Multi Professional Services
Mortimer Hill
Mortimer
Reading Berkshire RG7 3PG
(0734) 333070
Contact: Mr C. Dodson

Hoare, Lea and Partners
3—8 Redcliffe Parade
West Bristol BS1 6SN
(0272) 298811
Contact: Mr S. Edwards

George Kasabov
23 Stratford Villas
London NW1
(01) 267 3860
Contact Mr G. Kasabov

Ralph M Lebens
8 Paddington Street
London W1
(01) 487 2641

SLC Energy Group
125 Camberwell Road
London SE5 0HB
(01) 701 0326/7
Contact: Miss M. Ince

Solar Energy Developments
Bay 8
16 South Wharf Road
London W2 1PF
(01) 402 3202
Contact: Mr R. Francis

Robert Todd
National Centre for Alternative Technology
Llwyngwern Quarry
Machynlleth
Wales
(0654) 2400

Brenda and Robert Vale
The Horse and Gate
Witcham Toll
Sutton near Ely
Cambridgeshire
(035 377) 8723

John Willoughby
89 Prestbury Road
Cheltenham
Gloucestershire

Appendices

FUEL PRICE INCREASES

Since 1973, the *real* price of fuels has risen steeply, after a comparatively stable time during the previous decade.

The table below shows that the price of fuels in Britain has risen at a faster rate than the general level of inflation. From the period 1973 to 1977, the *real* cost of delivered heat has risen approximately 4.5% per annum for coal, 8.5% per annum for heating oil, 7.0% per annum for electricity, while the *real* cost of gas has fallen by 3.0% per annum. This declining price of gas in Britain is due to the marketing policy of the British Gas Corporation, but it should be noted that the price of piped gas in Britain is approximately half that of most European countries [1].

		1970	1971	1972	1973	1974	1975	1976	1977
COAL	Price per cwt[2]	85	98	107	108	133	175	206	246
	Real price per cwt[3]	85	90	91	84	90	96	97	99
	365 kWh/cwt @ 52% eff[4]	190	190	190	190	190	190	190	190
	Real price per kWh deliv.	0.45	0.47	0.48	0.44	0.47	0.50	0.51	0.52
OIL	Price per gall.[2]	9.54	10.67	11.42	15.42	23.00	29.50	37.28	39.19
	Real price per gall.[3]	9.54	9.79	9.76	11.95	15.54	16.12	17.50	15.80
	48 kWh/gall. @ 65% eff.[4]	31.2	31.2	31.2	31.2	31.2	31.2	31.2	31.2
	Real price per kWh deliv.	0.31	0.31	0.31	0.38	0.50	0.52	0.56	0.51
ELECTRICITY	Price per kWh (5000 kWh/p.a.)[2]	0.95	1.07	1.12	1.20	1.54	2.21	2.61	2.95
	Real price per kWh[3]	0.95	0.98	0.96	0.93	1.04	1.21	1.22	1.19
	1 kWh/kWh @ 95% effic.[4]	0.95	0.95	0.95	0.95	0.95	0.95	0.95	0.95
	Real price per kWh deliv.	1.00	1.03	1.01	0.98	1.09	1.27	1.28	1.25
GAS	Price per therm (400 therm/yr)[2]	11.08	12.35	12.96	12.96	13.37	17.70	19.60	21.20
	Real price per therm[3]	11.08	11.33	11.07	10.05	9.03	9.67	9.20	8.55
	29.3 kWh/therm @ 56% effic.[4]	16.4	16.4	16.4	16.4	16.4	16.4	16.4	16.4
	Real price per kWh deliv.	0.68	0.69	0.68	0.61	0.55	0.59	0.56	0.52

[1] *Eurostat:* Survey of Retail Prices: 1975

[2] **Digest of United Kingdom Energy Statistics.** Price in new pence.

[3] Fuel prices deflated by the RPI for all items excluding fuel, base 1970

[4] Szokolay, S.V. *Solar Energy and Buildings.* Architectural Press, 1975. p122

APPENDIX E

FUEL EQUIVALENTS

The figures below are approximate, but represent the orders of magnitude involved.

FUELS (large scale)

1 kWh of electricty contains	1	kWh
1 cubic metre of natural gas contains	11	kWh
1 barrel of crude oil contains	1700	kWh
1 ton of coal contains	7500	kWh

FUELS (domestic scale)

1 gallon of petrol (about 4½ litres) contains	48	kWh
1 gallon of paraffin (about 4½ litres) contains	46	kWh
1 therm of natural gas contains	29	kWh
1 14.5 kg cylinder of LPG contains	200	kWh
1 cwt of bituminous coal GP2 contains	423	kWh
1 three-bar radiator used for eight hours uses	24	kWh

APPENDIX F

ENERGY CONSUMPTION RATES

The figures below are approximates, but represent the orders of magnitude involved.

HUMAN CONSUMPTION RATES

The average well fed western man eats each day	3 kWh
The average manual worker produces each day	½ kWh
The average Ethiopian uses each year	300 kWh
The average Pakistani uses each year	1300 kWh
The average Briton uses each year	47000 kWh
The average American uses each year	100,000 kWh

OTHER CONSUMPTION RATES

The average domestic hot water unit uses each year	2000–5000 kWh
A return flight to Majorca for a couple consumes in aviation fuel	2500 kWh
The average house uses in space heating each year	4000–15000 kWh
A one-way flight from London to Melbourne for one person consumes in aviation fuel	10000 kWh
A 40 m^2 solar collector angled at 45° in London facing due south receives each year	40000 kWh
Operating at 30%, the above collector could deliver each year	13000 kWh
One large coal-fired power station (1000 MW) produces each year	8,800,000,000 kWh
The total UK consumes each year	2,640,000,000,000 kWh
The UK receives in solar radiation each year	232,500,000,000,000 kWh

Appendices

APPENDIX G

TEMPERATURES

THE SUN 5800 $^{\circ}$C

THE EARTH
Surface Approximates to air temperature
Two metres down Approximates to average yearly air temperature

WATER
Cold water 5–10 $^{\circ}$C
Luke warm water 30 $^{\circ}$C
Bath water 40 $^{\circ}$C
Kitchen sink water 50 $^{\circ}$C
Hot tap water 55 $^{\circ}$C
DHW cylinder water 55–60 $^{\circ}$C

SWIMMING POOLS
Before people will enter 20 $^{\circ}$C
Enjoyable 25 $^{\circ}$C
Preferable 30 $^{\circ}$C

LIQUID FLAT PLATE COLLECTORS
Average winter temperature of liquid 30 $^{\circ}$C
Average summer temperature of liquid 80 $^{\circ}$C
Temperature in summer if no liquid up to 185 $^{\circ}$C

AIR FLAT PLATE COLLECTORS
Collector air entering store 85° – 40°C
Store air entering house 40° – 60°C

HEATERS
Water in under floor tubes to
give 20°C air temperature
 (i) with tiles 24 $^{\circ}$C
(ii) with carpet 27 $^{\circ}$C
Water in fan convectors 40 $^{\circ}$C
Water in normal sized radiators 80 $^{\circ}$C
Water in oversized radiators 50° – 60°C

BODY
Skin temperature 31–34 $^{\circ}$C
Blood temperature 36.8 $^{\circ}$C

APPENDIX H

HEAT CAPACITIES

	kWh/m^3°C	Mj/m^3°C
Air	0.00033	0.00012
Aluminium	0.688	2.478
Bricks	0.462	1.67
Brass	0.921	3.34
Bronze	1.036	3.73
Concrete	0.596	2.15
Fireclay Bricks	0.417	1.50
Rock Store	0.276	1.00
Water	1.173	4.22
Wood	0.33–0.50	1.19–1.81

APPENDIX I

S. I. UNIT PREFIXES

Factor	Prefix	Symbol
10^{15}	Peta	P
10^{12}	Tera	T
10^{9}	Giga	G
10^{6}	Mega	M
10^{3}	kilo	k
10^{2}	hecto	h *
10	deca	da *
10^{-1}	deci	d *
10^{-2}	centi	c *
10^{-3}	milli	m
10^{-6}	micro	μ
10^{-9}	nano	n
10^{-12}	pico	p
10^{-15}	femto	f
10^{-18}	atto	a

* not recommended

APPENDIX J

CONVERSION FACTORS

LENGTH	MULTIPLY	BY	TO OBTAIN
	inches	25.4	millimetres
	inches	2.54	centimetres
	feet	0.3048	metres
	yards	0.9144	metres
	chains	20.1168	metres
	miles	1.609	kilometres
	millimetres	1000.00	micrometres (μm)

AREA	MULTIPLY	BY	TO OBTAIN
	sq. inches	645.2	sq. millimetres
	sq. inches	6.452	sq. centimetres
	sq. feet	0.0929	sq. metres
	sq. yards	0.8361	sq. metres
	acres	4046.9	sq. metres
	acres	0.4047	hectares
	sq. miles	2.590	sq. kilometres
	sq. miles	259.0	hectares
	hectares	10000.0	sq. metres

VOLUME	MULTIPLY	BY	TO OBTAIN
	cu. inches	16390.0	cu. millimetres
	cu. inches	16.39	cu. centimetres
	cu. inches	16.39	millilitres
	cu. inches	0.0164	litres
	cu. feet	0.0283	cu. metres
	cu. feet	28.32	litres
	cu. yards	0.7646	cu. metres
	cords	3.625	cu. metres
	barrels of oil	159.0	litres
	cu. metres	1000.0	litres

CAPACITY	MULTIPLY	BY	TO OBTAIN
	fluid oz. (UK)	28.413	millilitres
	fluid oz. (US)	29.507	millilitres
	pints (UK)	0.568	litres
	pints (US)	0.47	litres
	quarts (UK)	1.137	litres
	quarts (US)	0.946	litres
	gallons (UK)	4.546	litres
	gallons (US)	3.785	litres
	barrels of oil	159.0	litres

VELOCITY	MULTIPLY	BY	TO OBTAIN
	feet/sec.	0.3048	metres/sec.
	feet/min.	0.0051	metres/sec.
	m.p.h.	1.609	kilometres/hr.
	knots	1.853	kilometres/hr.

VOLUME RATE OF FLOW	MULTIPLY	BY	TO OBTAIN
	cu. feet/sec.	0.0283	cu. metres/sec.
	cu. feet/min	0.000472	cu. metres/sec.
	cu. feet/min.	0.4719	litres/sec.

MASS	MULTIPLY	BY	TO OBTAIN
	grains	0.065	grams
	carat	0.2	grams
	ounces	28.35	grams
	pounds	0.4536	kilograms
	stones	6.35	kilograms
	cwt.	50.80	kilograms
	kips	453.59	kilograms
	tons (imperial)	1.016	tonnes
	tons (imperial)	1016.05	kilograms
	short tons (US)	0.9072	tonnes
	tonnes	1000.00	kilograms

MASS RATE OF FLOW	MULTIPLY	BY	TO OBTAIN
	pounds/hr	0.000126	kilograms/sec
	pounds/min.	0.00756	kilograms/sec.

Appendices

Category	MULTIPLY	BY	TO OBTAIN
DENSITY	pounds/cu. inch	27.68	grams/cu. centimetre
	pounds/cu. foot	16.02	kilograms/cu. metre
	pounds/cu. yard	0.5933	kilograms/cu. metre
WEIGHT OF WATER	gallon (UK) of water	10.02	pound
	gallon (UK) of water	4.545	kilograms
	cc of water	1.0	grams
	litre of water	1.0	kilograms

TEMPERATURE

$$\text{deg. F} \times \frac{5(\text{deg. F} - 32)}{9} = \text{deg. C}$$

$$\text{deg. C} \times \left(\frac{9\,\text{deg. C}}{5} + 32\right) = \text{deg. F}$$

$$\text{scale deg. F} \times \frac{5}{9} = \text{scale deg. C}$$

Category	MULTIPLY	BY	TO OBTAIN
PRESSURE	pounds/sq.inch	703.069	mm of water pressure
	pounds/sq. inch	6895.0	Newtons/sq. metres
	pounds/sq. inch	70.3	grams/sq. centimetre
	pounds/sq. foot	47.88	Newtons/sq. metre
	tons/sq. foot	107252.0	Newtons/sq. metre
	feet of water gauge	2989.0	Newtons/sq. metre
	inches of mercury	3386.39	Newtons/sq. metre
	atmospheres	101325.0	Newtons/sq. metre
	millibars	100.0	Newtons/sq. metre
	bars	100000.0	Newtons/sq. metre
	meters of water gauge	9807.0	Newtons/sq. metre
	Pascal	1.0	Newtons/sq. metre
FORCE	pound force	4.448	Newtons
	Newtons	1.0	kilograms metre/sec^2
	Newtons	100000.0	dynes

Category	MULTIPLY	BY	TO OBTAIN
ENERGY	foot pounds	0.000376	watt hours
	foot pounds	0.324	calories
	foot pounds	1.36	joules
	BTU	0.000293	kilowatt hours
	BTU	0.29307	watt hours
	BTU	252.0	calories
	BTU	1055.06	joules
	Therms	29.307	kilowatt hours
	Therms	105.506	megajoules
	horsepower-hour	0.7457	kilowatt hours
	joules	0.000278	watt hours
	kilojoules	0.000278	kilowatt hours
	Megajoules	277.8	watt hours
	Gigajoules	277.8	kilowatt hours
	kilowatt hours	859000.0	calories
	calories	4.1868	joules
POWER	BTU/hour	0.293	watts
	horsepower	745.7	watts
	horsepower (metric)	735.5	watts
	horsepower	1.014	horsepower (metric)
	1 ton refrigeration	3.517	kilowatts
	watts	1.0	joules/sec.
	kilocalories/hour	1.163	watts
	calories/sec.	4.1868	watts
	kilocalories/min	0.0194	watts
INTENSITY (Density of Power)	BTU/sq. foot hour	3.155	watts/sq. metre
	Langleys/hour	11.63	watts/sq. metre
	Langleys/min.	0.0698	watts/sq. centimetre
	kilocalories/sq.m.hr	1.163	watts/sq. metres
	calories/sq.cm.hr	1.0	langleys/hour
	calories/sq.cm.hr	41.87	kilojoules/sq. m. hr.
	calories/sq.cm.hr	11.63	watts/sq. metres
THERMAL CAPACITY	BTU/deg.F	0.5275	watt hours/deg.C
	BTU/deg.F	0.0005275	kilowatt hour/deg. C

MULTIPLY	BY	TO OBTAIN
SPECIFIC BTU/pound deg.F	4.187	kilojoules/kg. deg. C
HEAT and BTU/cu.foot deg.F	0.0677	Megajoules/cu.m.deg.C
HEAT CAPACITY BTU/cu.foot deg.F	0.0188	kilowatt hours/cu.m. deg.C

	MULTIPLY	BY	TO OBTAIN
THERMAL	BTU inch/sq.foot		
CONDUCTIVITY	hour deg.F	0.144	watts/metre deg. C
(k value)	BTU/foot hr. deg.F	1.731	watts/metre deg. C
THERMAL	sq. foot hr. deg.F/		
RESISTIVITY	BTU/inch	6.944	metre deg.C/watt
(r value: $= \frac{1}{K}$)	foot hr. deg.F/BTU	0.578	metre deg.C/watt
THERMAL	sq. foot hr. deg. F/		
RESISTANCE	BTU	0.176	sq. metres deg. C/ watt
(R value)			
THERMAL			
TRANSMITTANCE			
(U-value: $U = \frac{1}{R}$)	BTU/sq. foot hr. deg. F	5.678	watts/sq. metre deg.C
LATENT HEAT	BTU/pound	2326.0	joules/kilogram
	BTU/cu. foot	37.26	kilojoules/cu. metre
	BTU/cu. foot	0.01036	kilowatt hours/cu. m.
	BTU/gallon	232.0	kilojoules/cu. metre

GAUGE

Gauge No.	SWG in.	mm
7/0	.500	12.70
6/0	.464	11.79
5/0	.432	10.97
4/0	.400	10.16
3/0	.372	9.45
2/0	.348	8.84
0	.324	8.23
1	.300	7.62
2	.276	7.01
3	.252	6.40
4	.232	5.89
5	.212	5.38
6	.192	4.88
7	.176	4.47
8	.160	4.06
9	.144	3.65
10	.128	3.25
11	.116	2.95
12	.104	2.64
13	.092	2.34
14	.080	2.03
15	.072	1.83
16	.064	1.63
17	.056	1.42
18	.048	1.22
19	.040	1.01
20	.036	0.91
21	.032	0.81
22	.028	0.71
23	.024	0.61
24	.022	0.56
25	.020	0.51
26	.018	0.46
27	.0164	0.42
28	.0148	0.38
29	.0136	0.35
30	.0124	0.31
31	.0116	0.29
32	.0108	0.27
33	.0100	0.25
34	.0092	0.23
35	.0084	0.21

Glossary

Absorbent: the less volatile of two working fluids used in an absorption cooling system.

Absorber Plate: a black surface in a solar collector that absorbs solar radiation and converts it to heat energy.

Absorptance: a coefficient (a) calculated by the ratio of solar radiation absorbed by a surface to the amount that strikes it. The balance is reflected. The reflectance coefficient (r) and absorptive coefficient (a) always equal one : $a + r = 1$.

Absorption Cooling: an air-conditioning method that uses solar-heated liquid to activate a cooling process.

Active System: a solar assisted heating or cooling system that uses external energy to transport heat between the collector, the store and the room space.

a/e ratio: a measure of the selectivity of absorber surfaces, defined by the ratio of absorptance to emittance at the operating temperature.

Air-type Collector: a solar collector that uses air as the heat transfer fluid.

Altitude: the angle between the horizon and the sun.

Ambient Temperature: the surrounding temperature.

Ampere (Amp): a unit of electric current commonly analogized with the volume of water flowing through a pipe.

Ampere-hour (Amp-hr): a measure of current over time. Battery storage capacity is often expressed in amp-hrs. A 100 amp-hr battery can store sufficient energy to release 1 amp for 100 hours. 10 amps for ten hours. 100 amps for 1 hour, etc.

Array: a bank or set of solar modules or collectors.

ASHRAE: an abbreviation for the American Society of Heating, Refrigeration and Airconditioning Engineers Inc. at 345E 47th Street, New York, NY 10017.

Autarchic: self sufficient and when applied in architecture meaning independent of all mains services.

Auxiliary Heat: the extra heat provided in a solar assisted heating system by a conventional heating system.

Azimuth: the angle between true south and a point on the horizon directly below the sun (for northern latitudes only).

Beadwall: a patented movable insulation system developed by David Harrison of Zomeworks Corporation that blows tiny polystyrene beads between two sheets of glass about 50 mm apart and removes them from the bottom by using an adapted vacuum cleaner.

Berm: man made earth banking against a building's wall to increase the insulation and deflect heat-robbing winds.

Blocking Diode: a device which allows electric current to flow in only one direction through it. Used in solar electric systems to keep batteries from discharging through the solar cells when their output is too low to be charging the system.

Bioconversion: the conversion of solar energy into chemically stored energy through biological processes.

Black Body: an ideal body that will absorb all radiation falling upon it and reflect none.

BTU or British Thermal Unit: the quantity of heat required to raise the temperature of one pound of water through $1^{\circ}F$.

Calorie: the quantity of heat required to raise the temperature of one gram of water through $1^{\circ}C$.

Chimney Effect: the tendency of heated air to rise (because of its lower density), an effect emphasised particularly when the air is constricted in a chimney.

Clerestory: a vertical window placed high in the wall near the ceiling.

Closed Loop: a system where fluid in a pipe (immersed in another fluid) circulates independently and in isolation to the other fluid.

Coefficient of Performance: a coefficient used to measure the effectiveness of heat pumps or refrigerators, and is the ratio of heat energy delivered to electrical energy used to drive the machine.

Collection: the act of trapping solar radiation and converting it to heat.

Collector: any device that collects solar radiation and converts it to heat.

Collector Angle: the angle between the collector and the horizontal.

Collector Efficiency: the ratio of usable heat energy supplied by the collector to the solar radiation striking the collector for a given period (instantaneous, daily, annual).

Concentrating Collector: a device that focuses the solar radiation onto a smaller area.

Concentration Ratio: the ratio of the collector area exposed perpendicular to the sun when compared with the smaller area of collector onto which the focussed radiation falls.

Concentrator Cell: a solar cell designed to operate under highly concentrated sunlight.

Conduction: the transfer of heat within a material (usually a solid) by its molecular movement. It is measured by the coefficient (k).

Convection: the transfer of heat by a material (usually a fluid such as air or water) by the bodily movement of that material. Natural convection is self-generating (such as the motion of hot air rising).

Convective Loop: the continuous flow of a fluid in a circular path, that is powered only by heat being applied to one side of the loop.

Cooling Season: that portion of the year in some parts of the world when outdoor heat consistently makes indoor cooling desirable to maintain comfort.

Declination: the amount that the earth tilts on its axis relative to the sun. It is measured by the angle created by the noonday sun and the earth's equatorial plane. It varies from $+23^{\circ}27'$ to $-23^{\circ}27'$.

Degree Day: a unit representing a $1^{\circ}C$ deviation in the mean daily outside temperature, when compared with a fixed temperature (in Britain $15.5^{\circ}C$). A summation of all these deviations for all the days of the heating season gives a degree day total which is used to calculate a building's heating requirement.

Design Heat Load: the instantaneous heat load for the most severe conditions.

Design Temperature: the lowest expected outdoor temperature for a location used to calculate the design heat load.

Differential Thermostat: an automatic device that senses the difference in temperatures between several components (i.e. the collector, the thermal store, the room space) and directs the flow of heat energy correctly.

Diffuse Radiation: solar radiation that is scattered by air molecules, dust and water vapour and other particles, so that it appears to come from the entire sky, as on a hazy or overcast day.

Direct Gain: a passive heating system that allows solar radiation to penetrate straight into the building via the windows, and heat the room space directly.

Direct Radiation: solar radiation that comes straight from the sun and is capable of casting a shadow.

Double Glazed: a surface that is covered with two close fitting (about 20 mm apart) glass panes or other similar transparent glazing material.

Drain-down: a facility of an open loop liquid system in which the liquid can be drained out of the collectors when freezing conditions appear imminent.

Drum Wall: a thermal storage wall which can be made by stacking 55 gallon drums of water one on top of the other, usually horizontally and one drum deep (see also *water wall*).

Emissivity: the ratio of the radiation emitted by a body to that which would be emitted by an ideal black body the same temperature and under identical conditions.

Emittance: a coefficient (e) that measures emissivity. It varies from 0.05 for polished metals to 0.96 for flat black paint. For the same wavelength, absorptance (a) equals emittance (e): a = e. But for the same material (a) and (e) may vary for different wavelengths.

Equinox: either one of the two times of the year when the day and night lengths are approximately equal. The autumn equinox is on or about September 22nd, and the vernal (Latin for spring) equinox is on or about March 22nd.

Eutectic Salts: a group of materials that absorb heat by changing from solid to liquid at a predetermined temperature (usually in the range of $25-50^{\circ}C$) and then release heat by changing from liquid to solid, again when the ambient temperature is sufficiently low.

Evacuated Tube Collector: a collector made from long concentric glass tubes, approximately the size of a fluorescent tube. There are many arrangements, but basically a small inner tube transports the heat transfer fluid, with an evacuated space between it and a larger outer tube.

Evaporative Cooling: a technique that cools air by passing it over a damp surface or a body of water.

Glossary

Flat Black Paint: a matt black paint that has a relatively high absorptance.

Flat Plate Collector: a solar collector with a flat plate as an absorber plate, rather than a device with a curved surface that concentrates solar radiation.

Flow Rate: the amount of heat transfer fluid (usually measured in cubic metres/sec. or kilograms/sec.) that passes through or over an absorber plate.

Forced Convection: the transfer of heat by mechanical means (fans, blowers or pumps) rather than by natural convection.

Freon: a volatile liquid capable of boiling at low temperatures and becoming lighter.

Glauber Salts: a eutectic salt of sodium sulphate ($Na_2SO_410\,H_2O$) that melts at $32^{\circ}C$ and absorbs about 315 Joules/kilogram.

Global radiation: the sum of direct and diffuse radiation measured on a horizontal plane.

Gravity convection: the natural circular movement of heat through a body of fluid, when the warm fluid rises and the cool fluid sinks.

Greenhouse effect: a heating effect created within an enclosed space by the ability of a glass or clear plastic surface to transmit the sun's shortwave radiation, but be opaque to the longwave radiation emitted back by the surfaces that have been heated by the sun.

Header: a horizontal pipe or duct at the bottom or top of a collector that distributes or collects the heat transfer fluid (usually air or water) to the individual pipes or ducts within the collector.

Heat capacity: see Specific heat.

Heat exchanger: a device to transfer heat from one fluid to another. There are three basic types: air/air, liquid/liquid and liquid/air. Air/air and liquid/liquid exchangers usually consist of long lengths of tubing, while liquid/air exchangers usually consist of a multi-finned length of tubing such as in a car radiator.

Heating season: a portion of the year (in Britain usually from September/October to April/May) when indoor heating is continually required.

Heat pipe: a device that transfers heat in one direction only and usually consists of a sealed pipe about 25 mm diameter and (say) 300 mm long. It heats up at one end causing a fluid inside to evaporate, travel to the cold end, condense, release heat, then return to the hot end either by gravity or by the capillary action of an internal wick.

Heat pump: a mechanical device that takes heat from one place (the heat source) and transfers it to another (the heat sink). The household refrigerator is such a device.

Heat sink: the place where heat is dumped by a heat pump (See Heat pump).

Heat source: the place from where heat is obtained by a heat pump (see Heat pump). Usually earth, air or water.

Heat storage: a material that stores collected solar radiation for re-release at a later time when required within the room space. The material can be water in cylinders, rocks in storage bins, eutectic salts in containers or just the building fabric itself.

Heat transfer fluid: air or liquid that is used to transport heat from one place to another (i.e. collector to store, collector to room, or store to room).

Heliostat: an electromechanical array of mirrors that tracks the sun's radiation onto a fixed point as the sun moves across the sky.

Hybrid system: a solar heating system that combines both passive and active systems.

IHVE: An abbreviation for the Institution of Heating and Ventilating Engineers, 49 Cadogan Square, London SW1: (01) 235 8548.

Incidence angle: the angle between the direction of the sun's radiation and a line perpendicular to the surface.

Indirect gain system: a solar heating system where solar radiation strikes a thermal storage wall that separates the room space from the outside. A generic term rather than a specific one.

Infiltration: the uncontrolled movement of outdoor air into the building through cracks around doors and windows, as well as walls, roofs and floors.

Infrared radiation: see radiation, infrared.

Insolation: the total amount of solar radiation — direct, diffuse and reflected — that strikes a surface exposed to the sky.

Glossary

Insulation: a material with a high resistance to heat flow. It is measured by "U-values".

Interseasonal store: a large body of very well insulated material that stores excess heat collected in the summer season for use during the winter season.

Isolated gain system: a heating system that collects solar radiation exterior to the room space, then transfers that heat into the room space when required. A generic term rather than a specific one.

Irradiance: radiant energy passing through unit area per unit time.

Irradiation: the process of being exposed to radiation.

Langley: a meteorologist's unit of measurement for solar radiation intensity. One langley equals one calorie per square centimetre.

Latent heat: the amount of heat energy absorbed per unit mass of substance when it changes state (either from solid to liquid or liquid to gaseous) without any change in temperature. It is measured in Joules per kilogram.

Life cycle costing: a method of cost analysis in which the operating, maintenance, fuel, depreciation and other costs are estimated for a given life time of a device and compared to the capital cost. It can therefore be used to compare systems that have different life times, running costs and capital costs, and is especially useful in comparing solar assisted heating systems (high capital cost and low running costs) with conventional heating systems (lower capital costs and higher running costs).

Liquid type collector: a solar collector that uses liquid (either water or a water/antifreeze mixture) as the heat transfer fluid.

Low grade energy: a term used in solar literature to define energy at a low temperature, such as the heat energy stored in the earth, the air or the ocean.

Magnetic south: the direction "south" as indicated by a compass.

Magnetic variation: the angular difference between magnetic south and true south, as defined by the stars.

Maximum heat loss: see peak heat loss.

Microclimate: the climate of a very small area, such as a building site. A microclimate may vary dramatically from the macroclimate (regional climate) in which it is situated because of variations in exposure, cloud cover, vegetation, soil, etc.

Movable insulation: a flexible form of insulation for windows so that the light and view can be retained when a high degree of insulation is not required. It can take the form of insulated shutters (both external and internal), roll-down quilt blinds, "Beadwall", etc.

Natural convection: convection that occurs naturally without the aid of a fan or pump. See gravity convection.

Night insulation: the same form of insulation as movable insulation.

Nocturnal cooling: the process of cooling a surface by exposing it to a clear night sky, the sky acting as an enormous heat "sponge".

Open loop: a system where the heat transfer fluid from the collectors feeds directly into the thermal store.

Parabolic reflector: a concentrating collector where the cross section of the absorber plate is a parabola with the tube carrying the heat transfer fluid at its focus.

Passive system: a solar assisted heating or cooling system that uses natural means to control the flow of thermal energy.

Payback period: the period of time a solar assisted heating or cooling system takes to recoup its higher initial capital costs (when compared with a conventional heating system) through fuel savings, lower maintenance, etc.

Peak heat loss: a measure of an instantaneous maximum rate of heat loss from a building. It is measured in watts or kilowatts. An average house may have a peak heat loss of 4000 to 6000 watts.

Peak Watt (Wp): referring to the maximum output of a system. A photovoltaic array capable under full sunlight of putting out 10 watts has a peak watt rating of 10. Under cloudy or hazy conditions its output will be considerably less.

Glossary

Percentage of possible sunshine: the percentage of daytime hours where there is enough solar radiation to cast a shadow.

Perihelion: the point in the earth's elliptical orbit when the earth is closest to the sun.

Photobiology: a biological subject that covers the relationship between solar radiation and biological systems.

Photochemistry: a chemical subject that deals with chemical reactions induced by solar radiation.

Photosynthesis: the conversion of solar energy to chemical energy by the action of chlorophyll in plants and algae.

Photovoltaic cells: a semiconductor device that converts light into electricity. The efficiency is usually measured in its ability to produce peak watts, that is one watt at a specified working voltage when under a solar irradiance of one kilowatt/square metre.

Power tower: (also known as solar tower). A tall tower, perhaps 500 m high, positioned to collect the reflected direct solar radiation from an array of heliostats. A heat exchanger at the top of the tower converts the working fluid into steam to drive a conventional steam powered electrical generator at the base of the tower.

Pyranometer: an instrument for measuring solar radiation both direct and diffuse. If mounted horizontally, it can be used to measure global radiation. The same instrument is often called a solarimeter.

Pyrheliometer: an instrument for measuring direct solar radiation only.

Radiant energy: energy transmitted as electromagnetic radiation.

Radiant panels: metal heating panels with integral passages for the flow of a heat transfer fluid. The room space is heated both by radiation and convection.

Radiation: radiant energy.

Radiation, infrared: electromagnetic radiation, whether from the sun or a warm body, with wavelengths larger than the red end of visible light (greater than 0.75 microns).

Radiation, solar: electromagnetic radiation emitted by the sun.

Radiation, ultraviolet: electromagnetic radiation, usually from the sun, with wavelengths shorter than the violet end of the visible light (less than 0.15 microns).

Reflectance: a coefficient (r) that measures the ratio of solar radiation reflected by a surface to the amount that strikes it. See also absorptance.

Reflected radiation: solar radiation that is reflected from objects on the earth (buildings, ground, etc.) onto a surface exposed to the sky.

Refrigerant: a volatile liquid used in refrigeration systems.

Relative humidity: the percentage ratio of the actual amount of moisture present in the air compared with the maximum amount of moisture the air could hold, at the given temperature.

Resistance heating: a method of electric heating that employs the natural convection of room air over bars that become hot because of their high resistance.

Retrofitting: the application of solar devices to existing structures or systems.

Risers: pipes that transport the heat transfer fluid in an upward direction, and connect header to header.

Rock storage system: a bin that contains fist sized rocks that absorb heat from solar heated air as it is forced through, and distributes heat to cool room air as it is forced through in the opposite direction.

Roof pond system: a passive form of heating and cooling that places the thermal storage mass on the roof in the form of bags filled with water.

Seasonal efficiency: a vague term that is sometimes used to measure the ratio of solar radiation effectively used inside a building to the solar radiation striking the solar collector.

Selective surface: a special coating applied to the absorber plate that absorbs most of the solar radiation striking it but emits very little thermal radiation. Such surfaces have high a/e ratios.

Semiconductor: a class of materials with a resistance to electric current between metals and insulators. In photovoltaic cells, it is used to absorb the solar radiation and convert it to electromotive force.

Glossary

Sensor: a device, perhaps 6 mm in diameter and 20 mm long, that is used to detect changes in temperature and relay that information to a control device. Also called a thermistor.

Shading coefficient: the ratio of solar radiation that passes through a particular glazing system to the total solar radiation through a single layer of clear double strength glass.

Shading mask: the two dimensional geometric description of the shading characteristics of a shading device. Once plotted it can be overlaid on a sun path diagram to determine the time of day and month of the year when the window will be shaded by the device.

Skytherm ^{TM} system: a patented roof pond system developed by Harold Hay of California that incorporates electrically operated horizontal shutters that slide across the top of the water bags to insulate them from the external environment.

Solar Belt Area: a geographical region where solar systems work extremely efficiently and are economically highly viable.

Solar constant: the amount of solar radiation that reaches the outside of the earth's atmosphere at the average earth-sun distance. It varies slightly, but has a mean value of 1.35 kW/m^2, with a normal variation of ±4%.

Solar fraction: (or solar heating fraction) the ratio of heat provided by the solar system to be the total heat requirement of the building. It can be a single month or a whole year fraction.

Solar furnace: a device used to achieve very high temperatures (in the range of 3,000°C) by the concentration of solar radiation.

Solar house: a house that derives at least 40% to 50% of its annual heating from the sun.

Solarimeter: see pyranometer.

Solar Cell: a photovoltaic cell designed specifically to produce electricity from sunlight.

Solar pond: a heavily salted body of water exposed to the sun that both captures and stores solar radiation since the stratified salt solution reduces heat losses.

Solar radiation: electromagnetic radiation emitted by the sun.

Solar assisted heat pump: a solar heating system that combines a heat pump with a conventional flat plate collector system. These two elements can be combined in three ways: in parallel, in series, and dual source.

Solar time: see sun time.

Solstice: either one of the two times in the year when the day and night lengths are most unequal. The summer solstice on or about June 22nd has the longest day of the year and the winter solstice on or about December 22nd has the shortest day of the year (in the northern hemisphere).

Space heating: the heating of AIR within a building.

Specific heat: a measure (Cp) of the amount of heat energy necessary to cause a 1°C temperature increase in 1 kg mass of a particular substance. It is measured in Joules/kilogram degree C. Of all the common substances, water has the highest specific heat of 4187 J /kg degC.

Sometimes volumetric specific heat is given (often called heat capacity) and it is then measured in Joules/cubic metre degree C.

Specific heat loss rate: an index of the thermal properties of a house, given as the total (conduction plus convection) heat loss rate per unit temperature difference. It is measured in watts/degrees C. An average house may have an index in the range of 200 to 400 W/deg.C.

Stagnation temperature: the high temperatures (150—200°C) that can be reached inside a collector on a clear sunny day when the heat transfer fluid is not circulating. This situation is not a desirable operating mode and represents a malfunction in the system.

Storage mass: see heat storage.

Stratification: in solar literature it refers to the formation of layered temperature zones within a substance. In a water cylinder hot water is stratified at the top, while in a rock storage system hot air is stratified at the air collector entry point.

Sun tempered: a building designed to benefit from the heating possibilities of the sun, though not necessarily enough to qualify as a solar house.

Sun time: the time of the day as determined by the position of the sun. Also called solar time.

Temperature zones: rooms grouped together in a zone that is characterised by a specific design temperature i.e. living, dining, kitchen at 21°C and bedrooms, bathrooms and halls at 17°C.

Glossary

Thermal admittance: the number of watts a square metre of surface will admit.

Thermal break (thermal barrier): an insulating material placed between two highly conductive materials to reduce the flow of heat. An air gap between two sheets of glass is a thermal break, as is the insulated core in metal window frames.

Thermal capacity: the amount of heat energy necessary to cause a $1^\circ C$ temperature increase in a body. It is measured in Joules/degree C.

Thermal inertia: the characteristic of a building with a large surface area of heavy materials, that damp out temperature fluctuations, thus maintaining a fairly constant indoor temperature despite changes in the outdoor temperature.

Thermal mass: the mass within a building that is used to store heat. Concrete floors, brick walls and water in containers are examples of thermal mass.

Thermal radiation: electromagnetic radiation emitted by a warm body. The warmer the body, the shorter the wavelength of that radiation.

Thermal storage wall: a wall with a high thermal mass (concrete, brick, adobe, water in containers) that stores solar radiation during daylight hours, then releases the stored heat at night when the temperature of the room has dropped.

Thermal Store: a material that stores heat. Water in cylinders or fist sized rocks in containers are examples.

Thermistor: see sensor.

Thermocirculation: the natural circulation of a fluid caused by the input of heat into one side of a closed system, thus causing the fluid on that side to become less dense and rise and be replaced by the denser colder fluid from the other side.

Thermosyphoning: see thermocirculation.

Tilt angle: the angle between the collector and the horizontal.

Time lag: the time taken for heat to travel through a thermal storage wall.

Transmittance: the ratio of solar radiation transmitted through a substance to the total solar radiation incident on that surface. Single glazing transmits about 85% of the total available radiation, while double glazing transmits about 75%.

Trickle type collector: a solar collector in which the heat transfer liquid flows down open corrugations in the absorber plate, rather than in tubes. It was popularised by Thomason in America and BRAD in England.

Trombe wall: a south facing masonry exterior thermal storage wall about 250 to 500 mm thick, faced with glass to create a gap (normally about 100 mm) between the glass and the wall. Heat is delivered to the room during the day by convection of room air, and at night by radiation and convection off the inside face of the wall. Popularised and developed by Professor Felix Trombe in France during the 50s and 60s, it was first patented by Professor E.L. Morse of the Lowell Institute in America in 1881.

True south: south as defined by the stars and not a compass.

Turbid atmosphere: an atmosphere containing dirt, dust, water droplets and other aerosols.

Turbidity: a factor describing the reduction in direct solar radiation caused by a turbid atmosphere.

Ultraviolet radiation: see radiation, ultraviolet.

Unglazed collector: a solar collector without a greenhouse effect. For low temperature applications (such as swimming pool heaters) the cost of glazing is often not warranted.

U-value: a coefficient (U) that measures the heat loss through a substance, taking into consideration the thermal resistance of the air films close to the interior and exterior surfaces. It is measured in watts/square metre degree C. A single glazed window has a U-value of about 5.5 $W/m^{2\,\circ}C$, while a cavity filled brick wall has a U-value of about 0.6$W/m^{2\,\circ}C$.

Viscosity: the resistance of a fluid to movement.

Visible light: electromagnetic wavelengths that are visible to the naked eye. They extend from 0.38 microns (the blue end) and 0.76 microns (the red end).

Waste heat recovery device: a device that captures heat from substances being expelled from the building (such as stale air or waste water). This heat is usually transferred to the incoming substances required to replenish the depleted supply (such as fresh air or mains water).

Water wall: a thermal storage wall constructed with vertical tubes of water, approximately 300 mm in diameter and occupying the full height of the room.

Weatherstripping: the act of reducing uncontrolled infiltration by caulking stationary gaps (window/wall joints, etc.) and providing seals to openable elements (windows, doors, hatches, etc.).

Zenith angle: the angle calculated by (90° — altitude).

Photograph Credits

All photographs by David Oppenheim except for the following:

Index

Index